Looking at Trauma

GRAPHIC MEDICINE

Susan Merrill Squier and Ian Williams, General Editors

Editorial Collective
MK Czerwiec (GraphicMedicine.org)
Michael J. Green (Penn State College of Medicine)
Kimberly R. Myers (Penn State College of Medicine)
Scott T. Smith (Penn State University)

Books in the Graphic Medicine series are inspired by a growing awareness of the value of comics as an important resource for communicating about a range of issues broadly termed "medical." For healthcare practitioners, patients, families, and caregivers dealing with illness and disability, graphic narrative enlightens complicated or difficult experience. For scholars in literary, cultural, and comics studies, the genre articulates a complex and powerful analysis of illness, medicine, and disability and a rethinking of the boundaries of "health." The series includes original comics from artists and non-artists alike, such as self-reflective "graphic pathographies" or comics used in medical training and education, as well as monographic studies and edited collections from scholars, practitioners, and medical educators.

Looking at Trauma

A Tool Kit for Clinicians

EDITED BY ABBY HERSHLER, LESLEY HUGHES,
PATRICIA NGUYEN, AND SHELLEY WALL

The Pennsylvania State University Press | University Park, Pennsylvania

Land acknowledgment language is drawn, in part, from that
developed by the Indigenous Affairs Office of the City of Toronto:
https://www.toronto.ca/city-government/accessibility-human-rights
/indigenous-affairs-office/land-acknowledgement/.

Library of Congress Cataloging-in-Publication Data

Names: Hershler, Abby, 1972– editor. | Hughes, Lesley, 1980– editor. |
    Nguyen, Patricia, 1994– editor. | Wall, Shelley, 1964– editor.
Title: Looking at trauma : a tool kit for clinicians / edited by Abby
    Hershler, Lesley Hughes, Patricia Nguyen, and Shelley Wall.
Other titles: Graphic medicine
Description: University Park, Pennsylvania : The Pennsylvania State
    University Press, [2021] | Series: Graphic medicine | Includes
    bibliographical references and index.
Summary: "Presents twelve trauma treatment models, accompanied
    by interactive comics, for use by clinicians and their clients.
    Includes instructions on how to use the models with clients;
    practical educational tips from professionals in the field; and
    references for further study"—Provided by publisher.
Identifiers: LCCN 2021023463 | ISBN 9780271092072 (paperback)
Subjects: MESH: Psychological Trauma—psychology | Psychological
    Trauma—therapy | Psychotherapists—psychology | Models,
    Psychological | Graphic Novel
Classification: LCC RC552.T7 | NLM WM 17 | DDC 616.85/21—dc23
LC record available at https://lccn.loc.gov/2021023463

We acknowledge that this book was co-created on the traditional territory of many nations, including the Mississaugas of the Credit, the Anishnabeg, the Chippewa, the Haudenosaunee, and the Wendat peoples, which is now home to many diverse First Nations, Inuit, and Métis peoples. We also acknowledge that Toronto is covered by Treaty 13 with the Mississaugas of the Credit and deeply appreciate the contributions that Indigenous peoples have made in shaping and strengthening both our province and our country as a whole. As settlers, we are grateful for the opportunity to meet here and we wish to thank all the generations of people who have taken care of this land for thousands of years.

Contents

Preface: Thinking Through Comics

Shelley Wall

This book demonstrates why "graphic medicine"—"the intersection of the medium of comics and the discourse of healthcare" (Czerwiec et al. 2015, 1)—is a rapidly growing field. Comics are a powerful and subtle medium and can offer a non-threatening point of entry into difficult topics; their value in patient education is increasingly recognized and documented (e.g., Green and Myers 2010; McNicol 2017).

Comics do not merely "illustrate" textual content; they transform it into a language that uses text and imagery to create a third thing. Time, for example, can be represented as space, as in chapter 6 ("Parallel Lives") in this volume; visual metaphors take the place of verbal descriptions, adding an affective dimension to an intellectual concept, as in the contrasting configurations of explicit and implicit memory in chapter 8 ("How Trauma Impacts Memory"). Metaphors, as Elisabeth El Refaie suggests, are "based on shared bodily and cultural experiences" and thus allow subjective, personal experience to be communicated to others (2014, 151). Artist Patricia Nguyen, in her narrative of the creative process ("From Concept to Comic"), documents the care that went into the choices of visual metaphor for this collection. Indeed, every aspect of these comics, from the choice of non-triggering imagery to the depiction of the human form, has been thoughtfully, iteratively developed and piloted with clinicians and clients at Women's College Hospital.

As a medical illustrator, Patricia Nguyen is a skilled visual storyteller. As a comics artist, she brings empathy and wit to the communication of sensitive and nuanced subject matter. Abby, Lesley, and Patricia's descriptions of their collaboration testify to the profoundly *synthesizing* nature of the comic form. They liken the process, too, to the process of therapy: moving from fragments (utterance) to wholeness (narrative). These comics represent the co-creation of meaning by many hands and minds.

And this co-creation does not stop with the publication of this book. Comics, like all texts, are inherently relational: they depend upon the active participation of the reader to make meaning. Scott McCloud, for example, notes the act of "closure" required by the reader to create connections between the panels of a comic (1994). Moreover, the pages that follow are not meant just to be read: they are a shared space for clinicians and their clients to make meaning together, and, through interactive invitations for clients to draw or write their responses in the spaces provided, they extend the circle of collaboration even further. It is our hope that this book will provide a place for shared creativity and healing and will be a model for future directions in trauma-informed care.

References

Czerwiec, MK, Ian Williams, Susan Merrill Squier, Michael J. Green, Kimberly R. Myers, and Scott T. Smith. 2015. *Graphic Medicine Manifesto*. University Park: Penn State University Press.

El Refaie, Elisabeth. 2014. "Looking on the Dark and Bright Side: Creative Metaphors of Depression in Two Graphic Memoirs." *a/b: Auto/Biography Studies* 29(1): 149–74.

Green, Michael J., and Kimberly R. Myers. 2010. "Graphic Medicine: Use of Comics in Medical Education and Patient Care." *BMJ* 340 (7746): 574–77.

McCloud, Scott. 1994. *Understanding Comics: The Invisible Art.* New York: Harper Perennial.

McNicol, Sarah. 2017. "The Potential of Educational Comics as a Health Information Medium." *Health Information and Libraries Journal* 34:20–31.

Acknowledgments

First and foremost, we want to acknowledge and thank our clients. To the many resilient, capable, and courageous people who have sought healing in their lives post-trauma, we see you and we thank you for allowing us to accompany you on part of your journey. Your commitment to reclaiming your boundaries and to experiencing your inherent value and worth has taught us more about humanity than we could have wished for in a lifetime.

This book would not have been possible without Shelley's Social Sciences and Humanities Research Council (SSHRC) Insight Development Grant that supported Patricia's initial contribution to this project while she was a student in the field of medical illustration. We also greatly value the support and encouragement of our colleagues (whom we also consider dear friends) in the Women's Mental Health Program at Women's College Hospital, as well as the brilliant trauma recovery researchers, trauma clinicians, and authors whose books and papers guide our clinical work and provided a blueprint for many of the models we share here.

Working together as a team of editors for the first time has been extremely rewarding. We want to acknowledge our appreciation for the opportunity to learn from each other and discover the benefits of interdisciplinary collaborations.

We are grateful to Char, Micah, Suzie, Marilyn, Ernie, Dan, Clara, Eden, Holly, Eva-Marie Stern, Anne Fourt, our extended families, and communities of friends. You have all been loving, patient cheerleaders the whole way.

To Kendra Boileau and the Penn State University Press team, we are in awe of your creative work and extremely thankful for your gentle guidance and enthusiastic support for this unique book. Your warm and thoughtful direction was a gift to us throughout the editing process.

Thank you to our reviewers Julie Blair, Lisa Plotkin, and those who remained anonymous, who took time out of their very full lives to thoughtfully share their expertise and feedback. Your passion for trauma therapy was palpable in every suggestion you made and we deeply appreciate your commitment to accessibility through comics. Thank you for your dedication to your clients and for the work you do.

And finally, to the clinicians who have purchased this book, we value your awareness and commitment to the principles of trauma-focused and trauma-informed care. We believe that incorporating these principles and fostering a culture of non-violence across healthcare organizations, education centers, communities, and other institutions will lead to improved health and well-being outcomes for all. We hope that these tools support you in your important work.

FROM CONCEPT TO COMIC

First, I meet with either Abby or Lesley so they can teach me about the model. My goal during these sessions is to figure out the main teaching points and how this affects the clients. After the therapy session, what should the clients have learned?

After our talk, I have these fragments of ideas that I need to piece together.

Although I can't say I have experienced the same traumas as the clients, I try to imagine how they may feel.

I start by trying to capture the feeling. How can I best represent feeling "trapped"?
There are many ways to represent the same feeling, which can affect the tone and message.

Sometimes I create mini comics for myself to understand the story behind the model. These aren't meant to be a draft of the model but simply a way for me to interpret what I learned from talking with Abby and Lesley. This helps me start to craft a narrative and think of how I would simply explain this model. It's also a start to creating some imagery that I could potentially use.

This is an example of a mini story comic I made for the Window of Tolerance model.

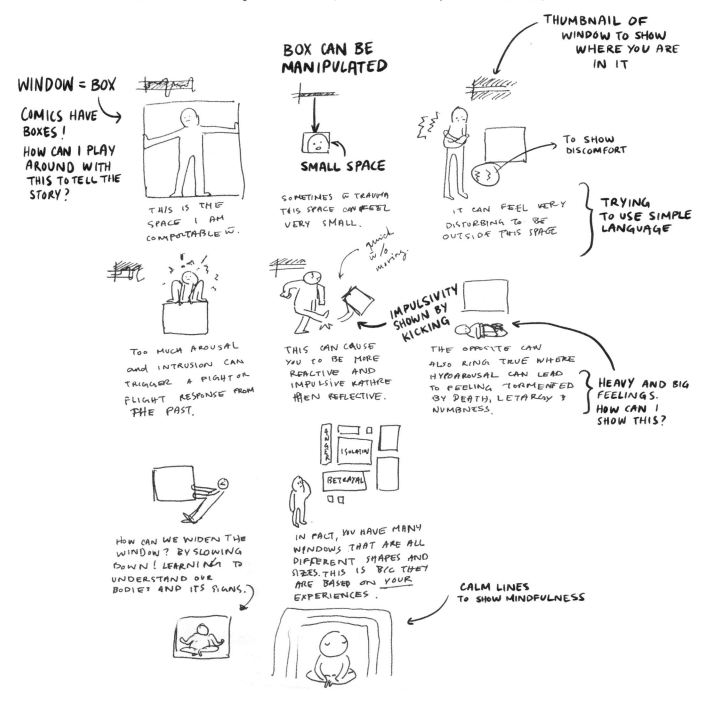

As with the mini comic, I often imagine myself explaining the model to a friend.

Another challenge is to think of neutral imagery that can invoke the same kinds of feelings associated with trauma without being triggering.

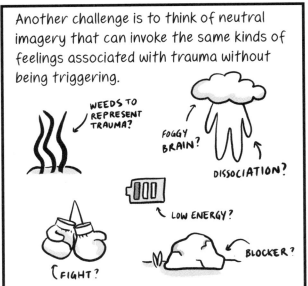

Slowly, I start lining up the pieces and building a story.

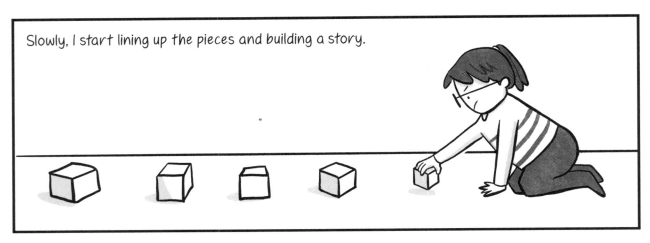

I then go back to Abby and Lesley to show them what I've come up with.

After the initial draft, there are lots of revisions to make sure we're staying true to the model and communicating the right information.

The models undergo a big transformation after I get my hands on them, and sometimes they stray too far from the original.

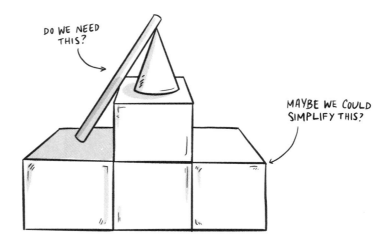

I am not a therapist. There is only so much I can interpret and draw into the model. Lesley and Abby are word wizards and know the model best. They are able to pick out details and refine the concept so that it best represents the original model and clients' experience.

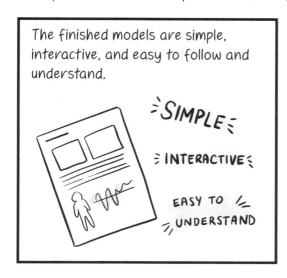

Thank you, Abby, Lesley, and Shelley, for always being so supportive, kind and encouraging.
Thank you for always going along with my wild ideas and teaching me so much along the way.
I, in my own way, have gone through a therapeutic journey with this project.

Introduction

Abby Hershler and Lesley Hughes

Experiences of childhood trauma contribute significantly to an increased risk of physical, social, and mental health problems across the life span. Unaddressed trauma can be passed on intergenerationally and epigenetically. While the personal impact of trauma is significant and life-altering, the problem is not only a personal one. Individuals, families, communities, and societies as a whole are affected by trauma, with the economic cost alone amounting to billions of dollars (Centers for Disease Control and Prevention 2020). Despite the barriers imposed by childhood trauma, we are repeatedly inspired by the resilience and determination of our clients. As trauma therapists, we have seen many people recover from childhood trauma and thrive, living creative, meaningful, and rich lives. In our work, we seek out tools and approaches to care that will support our clients' recovery. We are grateful for the education, evidence, advice, and supervision that we receive, and we feel indebted to the clients who have engaged in part of their healing process with us. We hope this educational tool kit is one way that we can contribute to resource building and developing community capacity. We have found these models to be valuable in our work as clinicians and educators, and we hope you will too.

Situating Ourselves

As two White Canadians, one born in Canada and one who immigrated there as an infant, we believe that being informed about the past and ongoing consequences of colonialism is vital to our work as clinicians. We are continuing to educate ourselves, and we encourage all of our readers to learn about the history of this land and to support Indigenous rights. We must be part of a collective commitment to actualize the calls for justice as outlined in the final report of the National Inquiry into Missing and Murdered Indigenous Women and Girls (National Inquiry into Missing and Murdered Indigenous Women and Girls 2019).

While writing this book, we have been living through the COVID-19 pandemic and a reckoning with historical and ongoing trauma, including anti-Black and anti-Indigenous racism, nationally and globally. This is happening on the heels of the explosion of Tarana Burke's #MeToo movement, resulting in countrywide and international dialogue about widespread gender-based violence and the lack of resources for survivors of sexual assault. The daily, ongoing impact of systemic racism and the intersecting experiences of oppression are central to every conversation we are having. We are also beginning to understand the traumatic effects of social isolation and physical distancing in response to COVID-19. There is a rise in opioid-related overdose deaths and domestic violence, as well as increased exposure to the SARS-CoV-2 virus and its physical and economic impacts for the most vulnerable in our community. We are striving to care for ourselves and each other—and becoming more aware of the resources needed to survive trauma in its many forms.

We are inspired by our clients and colleagues who have turned inward to examine the historical, societal, intergenerational legacies of trauma, suffering, and resilience. We are tremendously grateful for the opportunity to journey alongside our clients, to witness the depths of humanity, and to engage in this deeply meaningful work.

Background

We are a social worker and a psychiatrist working in the Trauma Therapy Program (TTP) and Women Recovering from Abuse Program (WRAP) at Women's College Hospital, an urban, academic, ambulatory care hospital in Toronto, Canada. We have worked with survivors of childhood trauma for more than a decade, and they have been our greatest teachers. We are in awe of our clients and their courage in the face of unjustifiable suffering, and we thank them for allowing us to accompany them for part of their recovery journeys.

This work would not be possible without the generosity of our TTP colleagues—both past and present—who have collectively translated their knowledge and experience over the years. We think about this program as a place where we have "grown up" as humans, one where each generation of clinicians adds to and develops the work of the people who have come before. Our predecessors created a culture that welcomes each therapist's experience and opinion, a culture that does not shy away from conflict or divergent perspectives. It honors the belief that collaborations lead to richer and more meaningful connections. We knew early on that we wanted to invite our colleagues in the trauma therapy team to author the chapters included in this book, certain that each person's unique perspective and approach to these models would enhance this publication. We are grateful that many of them agreed. We are thrilled that the clinicians who use this book will benefit from the knowledge and experience shared here.

Most of the models we share in this book were initially created and developed by our national and international colleagues who have significant expertise in the field of trauma therapy. We have translated our understanding of these models and adapted them in collaboration with Patricia Nguyen, a medical illustrator and comics artist extraordinaire. We recognize that our years of work with committed trauma therapy colleagues and the wisdom gained by working with hundreds of trauma survivors made this possible.

We were first introduced to Patricia by our dear colleague Eva-Marie Stern, an art psychotherapist who was a co-founder of WRAP over twenty years ago. Eva-Marie connected us with Shelley Wall, an associate professor of medical illustration with funding from the Social Sciences and Humanities Research Council to support a graduate student internship. Shelley hired

Patricia for a project dedicated to trauma education materials. Once we began co-creating and then using Patricia's comics in our clinical work, we wanted as many clinicians as possible, and their clients, to have access to them. This led us to Kendra Boileau at Penn State University Press, who became our mentor and cheerleader in the process of publishing this book. We are grateful for Kendra and her team's knowledge, warmth, and guidance in navigating this project.

As we were co-constructing the comics in this book with Patricia, we were forced to confront aspects of the educational models that we did not fully understand. We discovered that there were complex, interwoven threads of clinical and anecdotal experience that were foundational for our understanding of these models. Expressing this in words to Patricia proved challenging at times, as she needed us to be clear in order to translate the ideas into images. We spent many hours poring over the details of each model, often sharing ideas in fragmented ways—not unlike the experience that trauma survivors face when recounting their journeys. With Patricia's steady patience paired with her creative lens, our capacity to teach and explain the models expanded. We became increasingly aware of the value of illustration and comics and delighted in witnessing the evolution of these drawings each time we received a draft from Patricia. Looking back, it was an experience of having our complicated, fragmented, and sometimes indescribable ideas captured and reflected back to us simply and clearly, which parallels effective therapy.

Art making as a therapeutic tool is not new to us. However, the use of comics to increase the therapeutic impact of psychoeducation is a newer discovery for us. We have a growing appreciation for the value of illustrations and comics as tools for teaching and providing a framework for therapy. As well, we are increasingly aware of the importance of providing opportunities for our clients to draw. Drawing (images, colors, textures, or marks on paper) is a useful form of expression and one that some people find easier to access than words. It is a potential doorway to the unconscious and a way to express the inexplicable. We hope that clinicians and clients who use the models in this book will use drawing as a tool for reflection and discover its therapeutic value.

Our clients have expressed that people in their lives have felt frustrated and helpless when trying to support them. We have heard from clinicians who felt they had to refer clients elsewhere when they disclosed their trauma histories, because the clinicians didn't feel comfortable or equipped to treat trauma. We know that our own comfort in working with trauma survivors started with curiosity and an interest in learning about the impact of childhood trauma.

Over the years, we have witnessed how the simple intervention of psychoeducation can mitigate the heavy burden of shame and isolation that many trauma survivors experience. We have noticed physical changes, such as shifts in our clients' facial muscles and a straightening of their spines, as they learn about trauma and realize they are not alone. We have the heard words of appreciation when our clients express that they "finally feel understood," and tears of relief paired with grief as they come to terms with traumatic losses. We have challenged their resistance to compassionately reframing symptoms as normal responses to overwhelming events. Along the way, we have learned to soften, welcome, and appreciate this resistance as yet another survival strategy. We have seen how new knowledge and expanded resources allow individuals to regain control in their present lives, and to grow as creative, wise adults. As well, we have used these resources for ourselves. They help us as clinicians and humans address our own experiences of relational trauma, mitigate the impact of vicarious trauma, and enhance our overall well-being. We hope that this book will offer clinicians the tools they need to provide information about trauma to their clients and students in an accessible way.

We imagine this book as a collection of trauma education models with instructions—a psychoeducation toolbox. Each model provides a framework for understanding various impacts of trauma, to be drawn upon as needed. Each chapter (with the exception of chapter 1) begins with textual instructions written by one or two clinicians who specialize in treating individuals who have experienced childhood trauma. These textual instructions provide information about the model and step-by-step suggestions about how to use the comics and illustrations with individual therapy clients and in groups. As well, the authors end each chapter with educational gems and tips on how to deepen the use of these models in therapy.

The text is followed by an accompanying comic that is designed to be shared with clients and learners depending on the concerns or issues that are being discussed. The comics have been drawn with the intention of engaging clients in narratives that are accessible and relatable, with the aim of strengthening client-centered care. The reader will notice prompts designed to engage clients in tailoring their responses with words or images. We believe that inviting clients to capture their personal experiences is essential in supporting individuals with their growth and recovery aims.

We do not expect this book to be read linearly; each chapter is intended as a stand-alone educational aid. In some chapters, we have made suggestions when the content can be enhanced with information found in a companion chapter. With intention, the importance of reflecting on one's resources or self-care strategies is emphasized in each chapter. We do this as a reminder of the importance of pacing and ensuring a sense of safety and stability in one's body, thoughts, and emotions. Therapy is strong medicine and we promote titration to optimize the experience of learning tools for self-compassion and care throughout the healing process.

Chapter Outlines

We strongly believe that we can only support others if we start with ourselves, and therefore we are committed to self-care as a foundational step for healthy living, enhanced resilience, and the prevention of burnout. We have also seen the ways that parallel process occurs in therapy. By parallel process, we mean the ways that our relationships with ourselves and our colleagues are sometimes mirrored in our clients' experiences with each other in group or with us in individual sessions. We know it is essential that we address our interpersonal conflicts and tensions in peer supervision and do our own therapeutic work. We practice mindfulness and yoga, spend time in nature and with friends and family, use our holidays, attend therapy, and practice strategies for managing stress and conflict. And, of course, we sometimes struggle and do not get it right in relationships. We fall back on old unhealthy patterns for managing stress, and because there is no limit on self-care, we are always open to hearing new ways to take care of ourselves, and we are committed to highlighting the importance of this for others. For this reason, we have chosen to make "Care for the Care Provider" the first chapter of this book.

Fundamental to our approach to trauma recovery is the need for pacing and repeatedly returning to the safety and stabilization stage of trauma therapy (Herman 1997). Chapter 2 offers a framework for building resources for this first and essential stage of trauma recovery. This chapter discusses daily practices of self-care that support general health and well-being, and also recommends grounding tools for responding to immediate distress. Core to building new skills is honoring our clients' existing strengths and strategies for survival. We have purposefully located the self-care and grounding chapter toward the beginning of the book as a reminder that this work is foundational to subsequent work in trauma therapy and will need to be revisited by clinicians and clients throughout the course of therapy.

The neurobiological impacts of trauma including difficulties with emotion regulation, executive functioning, and interpersonal relationships are well-documented (Levine 2015). Chapter 3 provides an overview of complex posttraumatic stress disorder (cPTSD) and the constellation of symptoms commonly experienced by individuals who have survived repeated and chronic childhood trauma. While some clients have experienced diagnosis as stigmatizing, for others, it has been validating. An accurate and evidence-based diagnosis has the potential to allow for increased dialogue about the impact of childhood trauma, provide a starting place for research, guide treatment interventions, and allow clients to access resources and support when childhood trauma prevents them from engaging in full-time employment.

Long after traumatic events, individuals may find themselves unable to manage their physiological and emotional arousal. At the onset of treatment, clients often identify the wish to respond to situations in the present with a sense of control over their emotions, rather than feeling like they are caught in the past riding a roller coaster of feelings. Chapters 4, 5, and 6 provide models for understanding emotion regulation and dysregulation. Each model in this section provides a framework for understanding and normalizing attempts to regulate through tension-reducing behaviors (e.g., substance use, self-harm). While effective at the time, these behaviors often lead to significant shame and emotional distress, followed by further attempts to regulate. The "window of tolerance" model provides a useful scaffolding for reflecting on responses to daily stressors and how to build self-awareness and resources for stress management. Clients might discover that they can use the "trigger scale" model to tune into their thoughts, feelings, sensations, and behavioral impulses as indications that they need self-care and resourcing. Increased awareness may allow them to notice the signs that their past and present have collided; this can be explored more fully with the "parallel lives" model. The process of slowing down, noticing signs of emotional dysregulation, and using strategies to regulate and reconnect can be extremely beneficial in gaining a greater sense of control in daily life. These chapters emphasize the value of encouraging clients to be curious about themselves, as well as compassionate, as they expand their capacity for tolerating uncomfortable (but not dangerous) emotions and interactions.

In addition to emotional dysregulation, survivors of chronic trauma describe certain neurobiological impacts of trauma. For example, clients commonly report feeling that their executive functioning skills are compromised, particularly as these relate to attention and memory. Chapters 7, 8, and 9 discuss the neurobiological impacts of trauma and offer validation for common patterns of response to help clients separate their sense of self from symptoms of trauma. In chapter 7, we provide a simplified theory of brain functioning as it relates to trauma-driven reactions in the present and ways to expand prefrontal cortex self-regulation skills. In chapter 8, we explore how trauma impacts memory by differentiating between explicit memory—the experience of being present and remembering the past—and implicit memory—the experience of remembering the past through sensations, emotions, thoughts, and impulses. In response to childhood trauma, individuals often experience time as a continuous movement from past to future with very little sense of a present, and therefore, little hope that "this will end" (Lanius 2018). The "structural dissociation" model is included in chapter 9 to explore alterations in consciousness experienced during and after trauma, and the subsequent animal defense survival strategies common to trauma survivors (e.g., fight, flight, freeze, collapse).

When early childhood interpersonal experiences have been harmful, it is not surprising that relationship difficulties emerge as a symptom later in life. Clients describe a number of struggles, including avoidance in social situations, interpersonal conflict, and relationship instability. However, we believe that despite (or perhaps because of) these relational wounds, there is tremendous potential for healing through connection with others. Chapters 10, 11, and 12 provide ways of understanding relationship patterns that may develop as a result of trauma. "Karpman's triangle" and the "roles and re-enactment hexagon" models address the tendency for clients to find themselves unconsciously repeating patterns from their past in their present relationships. The "relationship grid" provides a framework for exploring boundaries and self-esteem in the context of relationships. All of these models encourage clients to notice unhealthy relationship dynamics and identify ways to shift these patterns. We hope that this will be a starting place for clinicians and clients to explore relational skills building.

Final Words

After many hours of collaboration, and a lot of personal growth, we are thrilled to present this book for clinicians in community and academic healthcare settings, with easy-to-use comics, illustrations, and text focused on the impacts of childhood trauma on the mind and body. We have chosen models that have been most useful to us in our trauma therapy work as well as those that offer a framework for learning new strategies for self-care and skills to respond to trauma-related symptoms in the present. We could not include everything, but we are pleased with what has been included, and appreciate the generosity of the original authors who have permitted us to use adapted versions of their work. We encourage clinicians to use each chapter as a springboard for learning and hope that they may be inspired to deepen their understanding of these models by seeking out the original sources. We also hope this material can be adapted or used in conjunction with the treatment of other types of stress, especially race-based traumatic stress.

We hope this book will be useful for all clinicians who wish to provide trauma psychoeducation to their clients, and educators who wish to provide trauma-informed and trauma-focused tools for their students. We aspire for the material in this book ultimately to benefit trauma survivors and the people who care deeply about their recovery.

References

Centers for Disease Control and Prevention, National Center for Injury Prevention and Control, Division of Violence Prevention. 2020. "Preventing Adverse Childhood Experiences." Last modified April 3, 2020. https://www.cdc.gov/violenceprevention/aces/fastfact.html.

Clark, Carrie, et al. 2015. *Treating the Trauma Survivor: An Essential Guide to Trauma-Informed Care*. New York: Routledge.

Herman, Judith Lewis. 1997. *Trauma and Recovery*. New York: Basic Books.

Lanius, Ruth. 2018. "Trauma and Altered States of Consciousness: Toward the Rebirth of the Self." Presented at the Trauma Talks Conference, Toronto, ON, June 8, 2018. http://www.traumatalks.ca/presentations2018/lanius.pdf.

Levine, Peter. 2015. *Trauma and Memory: Brain and Body in a Search for the Living Past; A Practical Guide for Understanding and Working with Traumatic Memory*. Berkeley, CA: North Atlantic Books.

Linklater, Renee. 2014. *Decolonizing Trauma Work: Indigenous Stories and Strategies*. Halifax, NS: Fernwood Publishing.

McKay, Matthew, Jeffrey C. Wood, and Jeffrey Brantley. 2019. *The Dialectical Behavior Therapy Skills Workbook: Practical DBT Exercises for Learning Mindfulness, Interpersonal Effectiveness, Emotion Regulation and Distress Tolerance*. Oakland, CA: New Harbinger Publications.

National Inquiry into Missing and Murdered Indigenous Women and Girls. 2019. *Reclaiming Power and Place: The Final Report of the National Inquiry into Missing and Murdered Indigenous Women and Girls*. [Vancouver, BC]: The National Inquiry. https://www.mmiwg-ffada.ca/wp-content/uploads/2019/06/Final_Report_Vol_1a-1.pdf.

World Health Organization and International Society for Prevention of Child Abuse and Neglect. 2015. *Preventing Child Maltreatment: A Guide to Taking Action and Generating Evidence*. Geneva, Switzerland: WHO Press.

Chapter 1

Care for the Care Provider

Marlene Duarte Giles

This chapter explores the impact that trauma therapy work has on the helper. In addition to exploring the ways we can be transformed by this work, we will also address the ways we are challenged—and what we can do to fortify and sustain ourselves. Caring for ourselves is of fundamental importance. This section notes areas that we deem essential for clinicians and care providers to reflect upon. Our own therapy, education, and self-care are foundational to this work.

Transference and Countertransference

The role of transference and countertransference in the therapeutic relationship has long been established. Transference in therapy is the redirection, to one's clinician, of emotions that were originally felt in childhood. Countertransference is the clinician's emotional reaction to their client that maps onto their own past experiences.

Transference is a "logical" extension of a client's childhood experience. The therapeutic relationship re-activates abuse memories where issues of power/authority, caretaking, and closeness come alive in the exchange between client and clinician. Transference can then be used as

an opportunity to re-process childhood issues. Transference must be addressed in order not to be taken personally by the clinician.

Additionally, clinicians must find ways to identify and articulate countertransference reactions—their response to their client's transference. Ideally, this happens through the support provided in supervision. Maggie Ziegler and Maureen McEvoy describe the intricacies of navigating countertransference reactions in trauma groups as a "hazardous terrain" (2000). Part of hazard management in therapy requires us to address our countertransference reactions—for example, by recognizing and resisting "the pull" to react to a client the way one might have reacted in a childhood relationship. We can also make use of countertransference reactions in the therapeutic relationship in a number of ways. We can reflect on the origin of our own reactions and how they relate to a client's history and childhood relationships. Relationship dynamics can then be discussed in therapy in order to shift repetitive, unhealthy relational patterns and foster new opportunities for growth. Countertransference provides an opportunity for clinicians to identify their self-care needs. Supervision and one's own therapy become important opportunities to explore countertransference and to process reactions outside of one's work with clients. Some commonly reported countertransference reactions from clinicians include:

- Feeling frustrated by clients who state that "nothing works" or that they "have tried everything."
- Feeling helpless when clients are "stuck," struggling to put skills into practice.
- Feeling incompetent and de-skilled when clients voice that they "are not getting better."
- Feeling compelled to rescue a client when a client seems ambivalent or disengaged.
- Feeling depleted by offering more time, support, and/or resources to the client; in essence, the clinician is working harder than the client.

Parallel Process

The models in this book can also be used by clinicians to assess their level of grounded presence when working with trauma clients. It can be helpful to begin by reflecting on the following questions: Are you inside or outside your window of tolerance? Are you practicing the stress management skills that you have recommended to your clients? Are you exercising, getting proper rest, eating nutritious meals, reaching out for support from family or friends, community resources, or healthcare professionals?

Vicarious Trauma

Those of us who work with clients and families who have experienced or continue to experience trauma are naturally affected by the stories that are shared in therapy. It is useful to reflect on our exposure to the re-telling of traumatic experiences and to strategize to reduce stress and prevent harm to ourselves. Stress, compassion fatigue, burnout, and vicarious traumatization are the occupational health hazards of a trauma clinician's work. It is important for healthcare providers to monitor the impact of the work on our physical, emotional, mental, relational, and social well-being. We recommend that you read more about ways to identify and protect yourself from vicarious trauma, compassion fatigue, and burnout. Leaders in the field of vicarious trauma have developed useful resources for frontline workers to assess the impact of their work (see References).

Co-facilitation Relationship

In cases of co-facilitation, it is important to prioritize the co-facilitation relationship and address the relational dynamics that arise between co-leaders when working on a team. One example arises when one co-leader is perceived as the caring, nurturing, idealized parental figure and the other co-leader is seen as the authority figure, limit-setter, or, in some cases, as a perpetrating figure representing someone from the client's past. This example and other re-enactments occur frequently and are important to identify and address.

Supervision

Reflective Debriefing

There may be little time in the day to carve out a formal supervision meeting. Taking ten to fifteen minutes before and after group is sometimes all that is needed. This small window can help co-therapists prepare material, highlight concerns, and divide the co-facilitation work in the group before the session, which can then be followed by a reflective debrief after the session. Student learners can also be invited to join in the debriefing; this experience can add rich learning about group planning, anticipating pitfalls, and building a collaborative co-therapy relationship. A brief conversation before and after each group is essential to maintain continuity of clinical care; to discuss current events in the client group; and to explore concerns, countertransference issues, and clinical themes raised in-group in addition to planning curriculum for future sessions.

Weekly Supervision

Formalizing clinical team supervision can look different depending on the work setting. We suggest setting aside ninety minutes weekly for the clinical team to come together for this purpose. This time can be divided up based on the needs of the team and individual clinicians—for example, addressing clinician needs, client needs, team health and functioning, and administrative issues. Issues pertaining to transference and countertransference can be explored, as well as interpersonal dynamics within the team such as co-therapy relationships. Peer supervision and support can also help mitigate the potential effects of vicarious traumatization, in addition to offering an opportunity to engage in case consultation and collaborative interdisciplinary treatment planning. In some cases, you may want to hire an external consultant with expertise in an area that may be missing in your team, such as psychiatry, or bring in an expert who specializes in using a particular modality.

If you work independently, consider creating a peer supervision group and hiring an expert or consultant to provide group supervision and support.

Self-Care

As a clinician with twenty-five years of experience, I have been asked countless times over the years, "How have you managed to do trauma work for so long?" The answer is self-care. It may seem like a simple answer, but in practice, it is far more difficult. You have likely heard your clients say that practicing self-care is an area of growth for them, that they don't know where to start or what to do. They may feel selfish or undeserving of setting aside time for themselves, and/or they feel guilty if they reward themselves or experience pleasure, especially in the face of others' suffering. Does this sound familiar to you? Is this similar to your own internal dialogue? As helpers, we are often learning what is best for us alongside our clients. We are modeling to our clients and co-workers that we value self-care.

Self-care for healthcare professionals can be broken down into several categories (Saakvitne 2001; Pearlman and Saakvitne 1995). Below you will find suggestions for strategies to support yourself, your team, your organization, your profession, and/or your community.

Personal Strategies

- Take "mini" breaks between sessions, such as going for a walk, taking a bathroom break, visiting with a co-worker, stretching, drinking a glass of water. I knew a therapist who would knit between sessions; over time she had a cozy assortment of sweaters.
- Take vacations. "Staycations" can also be restorative, seeing your city through the eyes of a tourist.
- Seek personal therapy.
- Get proper nutrition, rest, and exercise. Fuel your body throughout the day by making your own lunch and snacks, or go out for lunch with a co-worker.
- Personalize your office space with artwork, plants, and lighting.
- Communicate feelings. Find creative, expressive ways through writing, journaling, or art making.

- Find a new hobby or interest, like salsa dancing, bird watching, guitar lessons, or rock climbing.
- Enhance your relationship with your physical self. Pay attention to your senses, movement, and breathing.
- Enhance your relationship with your spiritual self. Explore values, beliefs, and rituals. Join a choir or a spiritual community that resonates with you.
- Nurture connections to friends and family. Celebrate milestones such as birthdays as well as personal and professional achievements.
- Understand your personal history of violence and develop the practice of self-compassion.

Organizational/Professional Strategies
- Ensure workload standards are manageable.
- Encourage collaborative work or shared work.
- Ensure institutional support for self-care (e.g., supporting part-time work or "self-care" days).
- Provide debriefing opportunities.
- Value connections to professional, community, and political organizations that support clinicians and their work.
- Develop and maintain standards, protocols, and best-practice models that integrate traumatic stress reduction and resolution opportunities.
- Seek professional/peer supervision that addresses empathic connection and provides educational and research opportunities.
- Establish unconscious bias training and build policies to address microaggressions.
- Practice critical allyship.

Community and Social Strategies
- Educate others; consider being a clinical supervisor to a future healthcare professional.

- Understand the link between socioeconomic risk factors and disease.
- Learn more about racism and other forms of discrimination, oppression, and inequity as they relate to accessing power.
- Work to promote health and wellness within the local community through coalition-building and joint projects.

Environmental and Political Strategies
- Reduce single-serve plastics use in your work area.
- Bring your reusable coffee cup.
- Fill your own water bottle at work.
- Review and actively participate in social and political debates that address relevant healthcare concerns.
- Attend to human rights violations that compound disease, violence, and oppression. Promote equity as it relates to gender, race, ability, age, culture, religion, sexual orientation, class, and immigration/refugee status (social determinants of health).

Trauma work can be equal parts demanding and rewarding. We hope that in caring for your clients, you also take the time to care for yourself. Start by bringing your awareness back to yourself with curiosity and compassion. Take time to reflect on your work and how it affects you on all levels—emotionally, spiritually, socially, mentally, and relationally. What are the positive or transformative ways your work affects you, as well as the challenging or depleting ways? Then ask yourself, "What do I need?" Meeting this need can come from within, or it can come from reaching out to others for support—family, partner, friends, and co-workers. It may also mean advocating for change on a systems or organizational level. Those who meet their own needs are often better equipped to meet the needs of others. Finding a balance between work life and personal life is part of our life's work. Hope for a better future, health, longevity, and reduced suffering is what we aspire to for our clients—why not for ourselves?

Self-Reflection Questions

· What types of clients do you find most challenging to work with?

· What supports do you need—or have found helpful—in working with these challenging clients?

· What types of clients do you enjoy working with?

· What conditions allow you to feel you can do your "best work" (e.g., office environment, proper sleep, time for administration)?

· How do you know when you are outside your window of tolerance? (See chapter 4.)

· What "hooks" you in the therapeutic relationship?

· What are your safety nets or soft places to land that help support you (e.g., supervision, self-care strategies when at work or home)?

· What are your self-care goals for the day? Week? Month? Year?

· What is a self-care strategy you have always wanted to try and haven't yet? Try it!

References

Duarte Giles, Marlene, Andrea Nelson, Felisa Shizgal, Eva-Marie Stern, Anne Fourt, Pat Woods, Judy Langmuir, and Catherine Classen. 2007. "A Multi-Modal Treatment Program for Childhood Trauma Recovery: Women Recovering from Abuse Program (WRAP)." *Journal of Trauma and Dissociation* 8(4): 7–24.

Figley, Charles R. 1995. "Compassion Fatigue as Secondary Traumatic Stress Disorder: An Overview." In *Compassion Fatigue: Coping with Secondary Traumatic Stress Disorder in Those Who Treat the Traumatized*, edited by Charles R. Figley, 1–19. New York: Routledge.

Freud, Sigmund. (1910) 2001. "The Future Prospects of Psycho-Analytic Therapy." In *The Standard Edition of the Complete Psychological Works of Sigmund Freud*, edited by James Strachey, 11:139–52. London: Random House Colchester.

Mathieu, Françoise. 2012. *The Compassion Fatigue Workbook: Creative Tools for Transforming Compassion Fatigue and Vicarious Traumatization*. New York: Routledge.

Pearlman, Laurie A., and Karen W. Saakvitne. 1995. *Trauma and the Therapist: Countertransference and Vicarious Traumatization in Psychotherapy with Incest Survivors*. New York: W. W. Norton.

Saakvitne, Karen W. 2001. *Relational Teaching, Experiential Learning: The Training Manual for the Risking Connection Curriculum*. Baltimore, MD: Sidran Institute Press.

Saakvitne, Karen W., Sarah Gamble, Laurie Anne Pearlman, and Beth Tabor Lev. 2000. *Risking Connection: A Training Curriculum for Working with Survivors of Childhood Abuse*. Baltimore, MD: Sidran Institute Press.

Saakvitne, Karen W., Laurie Anne Pearlman, and the Staff of the Traumatic Stress Institute/Center for Adult and Adolescent Psychotherapy. 1996. *Transforming the Pain: A Workbook on Vicarious Traumatization*. New York: W. W. Norton.

Ziegler, Maggie, and Maureen McEvoy. 2000. "Hazardous Terrain: Countertransference Reactions in Trauma Groups." In *Group Psychotherapy for Psychological Trauma*, edited by Robert H. Klein and Victor L. Schermer, 116–40. New York: Guilford Press.

Chapter 2

Self-Care and Grounding

Meaghan Peckham

Background

Self-care practices and grounding resources help clients build awareness of their needs and internal indicators of distress. This allows them to decrease distress, regulate arousal within the window of tolerance, stabilize trauma symptoms, and establish a sense of safety, competence, autonomy, and confidence in their lives (Ogden and Fisher 2014).

The experience of interpersonal trauma is one of having the perpetrator's needs met at the expense of one's own needs. "If children have primary attachment figures who are abusive, neglectful, or inconsistent, they tend to see themselves as unworthy of care and others as untrustworthy" (McCallum, Woods, and Hill-Mohamed 2018, 24–25). For clients who have experienced childhood abuse and/or neglect, engaging in self-care, soothing, and self-nourishing practices can be very challenging, as these practices can feel foreign and potentially unsafe.

Self-care is the daily practice of engaging with strategies, routines, and activities that assist in preserving or improving an individual's health

and well-being. This assists in maintaining an internal equilibrium and regulating arousal. Self-care is the practice of meeting basic needs as well as incorporating practices that attend to the emotional, physical, and spiritual aspects of health and well-being. When our needs are met, we have an increased capacity to tolerate stressors and diminish baseline distress.

Grounding strategies and skills are the tools that we call on to regulate ourselves when we are experiencing immediate emotional distress. These strategies can include external distraction techniques as well as strategies that tend to physical, sensory, and somatic experience(s) to regulate arousal. Grounding strategies incorporate self-regulation (ways we use ourselves for soothing) as well as interactive regulation (things we do in our environment or with another person). We can use these strategies when we are temporarily over-activated (hyperaroused) or under-activated (hypoaroused) to help us re-enter our window of tolerance (see chapter 4) and widen it over time.

How to Use This Model

Part 1: Self-Care

Start by explaining the definition of self-care:

- Self-care is the act of engaging in regular practices that meet needs connected to our emotional, physical, and spiritual selves.
- Engaging in resourcing allows us to preserve and enhance our well-being and cope with stress.
- Daily self-care practices help widen the window of tolerance and minimize reactivity.
- Self-care practices can fall into four categories: physical, spiritual, mental, and emotional.

Review the self-care tool belt illustration and examples. The skills and practices help build and maintain a foundation of health and well-being. Some tools get used regularly, and there is room to gain new tools and skills along the way.

Ask the client or group to brainstorm self-care practices they already engage in for each of the categories listed.

Part 2: Grounding

Start by describing the definition of grounding:

- Any activity, skill, or strategy that helps us feel calmer, centered, and connected to ourselves, our bodies, and the present.
- Grounding helps widen the window of tolerance and is used in times of immediate distress.
- Grounding is useful in turning down the brain's fight, flight, freeze, and collapse responses.
- Grounding activities include things we do without awareness, such as rocking, stroking our legs, running our fingers over our lips, or taking deep breaths.

Review the grounding first aid kit illustration and examples. The items in the first aid kit are available in times of acute distress. Their purpose is to temporarily distract and to decrease the intensity of the situation.

Ask the client or group to brainstorm grounding practices they already engage in for each of the categories listed.

Explain how a heightened level of activation can make it challenging to access grounding strategies. Ask the client or group what situations make it difficult to implement grounding techniques.

Ask the client or group to identify three new strategies they will practice between sessions.

Educational Gems

- Checking-in with self and building awareness of internal cues will assist in intervening before becoming overwhelmed.
- Acknowledge that it takes time and repetition to make self-care practices and grounding resources a habit.
- Experiment with different strategies at different times and levels of distress. This is useful in determining effective strategies in a variety of situations.
- Collaboration is essential. Always ask permission, suggest practices as experiments, and give clients menu options and choices about whether to say yes, no, or change their minds.
- For hyperarousal, body-based grounding strategies (e.g., physical actions, breath) help calm the brain and body.
- For hypoarousal, posture experiments (e.g., subtle alignment of the spine) help awaken the brain and body.
- Body awareness and connection do not always feel safe for clients. If the body is not yet accessible for the client, external grounding (e.g., naming objects of a certain color in a room) may be an easier place to start.

- There are lots of ways to be mindful. "Directed" mindfulness (e.g., mindful movement/yoga) brings one experience in the body into focus and can be helpful for hyperarousal; others prefer "general" mindfulness, which is mindful attention that isn't focused.
- Express an equal investment in what works and what does not work for your clients. Both are necessary for discovery and learning.
- Reframe and validate barriers to self-care in the present as strategies that have allowed them to survive in the past.
- Using a parts framework, draw on the wisdom of the adult self to see if there's a willingness to help distressed parts by engaging in grounding or self-care.
- Acknowledge internal conflicts related to resourcing: "One part of you feels hopeless and doesn't believe anything will help, while another part of you is eager to learn and get some relief."
- Celebrate complexity in the system as an opportunity for exploration and choice. This can lead to more self-compassion if clients understand that a variety of approaches will be required.

References

Cutler, Ame. 2018. "The Somatic Narrative in Treatment of Trauma: A Sensorimotor Psychotherapy Approach." PowerPoint presentation at the Trauma Talks Conference, Toronto, ON, June 8, 2018. http://www.trauma talks.ca/presentations2018/Cutler.pdf.

Fisher, Janina. 2017. *Healing the Fragmented Selves of Trauma Survivors: Overcoming Internal Self-Alienation*. New York: Routledge.

McCallum, Nancy, Pat Woods, and Bonilyn Hill-Mohamed. 2018. "Trauma and the Body: Understanding the Connection Between Attach Cry and Self-Care." PowerPoint presentation at the Trauma Talks Conference, Toronto, ON, June 8, 2018. http://www.traumatalks.ca/presenta tions2018/McCallum.pdf.

Menakem, Resmaa. 2017. *My Grandmother's Hands: Racialized Trauma and the Pathway to Mending Our Hearts and Bodies*. Las Vegas: Central Recovery Press.

Ogden, Pat, and Janina Fisher. 2014. *Sensorimotor Psychotherapy: Interventions for Trauma and Attachment*. New York: W. W. Norton.

van der Kolk, Bessel A. 2014. *The Body Keeps the Score: Brain, Mind, and Body in the Healing of Trauma*. New York: Viking.

SELF-CARE AND GROUNDING

As humans, it's important to take care of ourselves both physically and mentally.

I am enough

To do so, we have to practice and learn strategies to reduce stress and take care of ourselves.

GROUNDING FIRST AID KIT

SELF-CARE RESOURCING TOOL BELT

This task can be particularly challenging when people have experienced childhood trauma.

inhale...exhale...inhale

WHAT STRATEGIES CAN WE USE?
Here are two collections of resources you can build to support yourself in daily life.

SELF-CARE TOOL BELT
Strategies to use on a DAILY basis

Self-care helps widen your window of tolerance. You can make deposits into your self-care bank to fuel the mind, body and spirit.

GROUNDING FIRST AID KIT
Strategies to use in times of IMMEDIATE distress

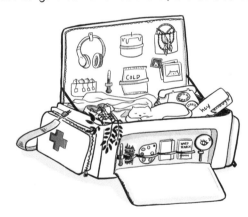

Grounding skills are helpful in difficult moments to turn down the brain's fight, flight, freeze and collapse responses.

GROUNDING: YOUR FIRST AID KIT

Grounding is a way to distract yourself from emotional distress. It is a collection of strategies and skills that allow you to move from HYPERarousal or HYPOarousal to a state of increased calmness and clarity. Grounding skills are like tools in a first aid kit. If you build your first aid kit in advance, it is more likely to be available to you in a time of distress.

PHYSICAL/SENSORY

- Place an ice pack on your wrists or splash water on your face or hands
- Hold an object in your hand (e.g., smooth stone, a squishy ball)
- Focus on your breath (e.g., belly breathing, pay attention to each inhale and exhale)
- Feel your feet on the ground
- Clench and release your fists
- Drink a comforting beverage (e.g., herbal tea)
- Smell essential oils or coffee beans
- Push against a wall

SPIRITUAL

- Read mantras, poems or religious texts that are meaningful to you
- Listen to spiritual music
- Use prayer in a way that works for you
- Create a nature scene in your imagination
- Listen to the words of a spiritual guide
- Connect with your experience of the divine or higher power

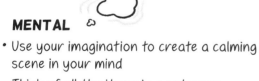

MENTAL

- Use your imagination to create a calming scene in your mind
- Think of all the items in a category (e.g., types of music, cities, vegetables)
- If you feel younger than your current age, identify the age you feel and count up to your actual age (in 2- to 5-year increments)
- Name all the objects in the room of a certain color
- Count backwards from 100
- Remind yourself of your name, age, date, location
- Describe your environment in great detail (sights, smells, sounds)

RELATIONAL

- Spend time with an animal
- Ask for a hug from a trusted person
- Call or text a friend (without expecting an immediate response)
- Say kind statements to yourself
- Look at photographs of people or animals whom you care about
- Place your hands by your heart and direct a loving thought to yourself (e.g., "I'm enough," "I deserve love")

BUILD YOUR FIRST AID KIT: WHAT GROUNDING TECHNIQUES WORK FOR YOU?

PHYSICAL/SENSORY 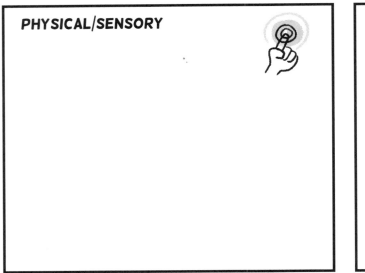	**SPIRITUAL** 
MENTAL 	**RELATIONAL** 

TIPS AND TRICKS FOR YOUR GROUNDING PRACTICE

1. Try out different types of grounding to see what works best for you. Talk to other people about what works for them and experiment for yourself.

2. Practice near your baseline on your trigger scale (not when you are distressed). This trains your brain and allows you to access grounding skills more readily when needed.

3. Commit to a daily practice (5–20 minutes). Choose a place and time to do this each day.

4. Rate your level of HYPERarousal or HYPOarousal prior to starting a grounding practice. Where are you on your trigger scale? Re-assess your level of arousal after grounding. This will help you identify which grounding skills are most useful for you.

5. Focus on the here and now (your present experience) rather than the past or the future.

6. Make a list of grounding skills that work for you (on cue cards, on your phone…) and refer to it regularly.

7. Keep trying! Like any new skill, learning grounding takes time and practice, as well as patience and self-compassion.

SELF-CARE: YOUR TOOL BELT

Self-care is a way to deliberately engage in activities to improve your mental, physical, emotional and spiritual well-being. Your tool belt is filled with a collection of strategies and actions that help you build a healthy foundation for moving through the world. This tool belt requires you to do a small amount of work on a daily basis. When you take care of yourself this way, you are widening your window for tolerating stressors and creating a baseline on your trigger scale that is closer to "0."

PHYSICAL/ SENSORY

Help you stay healthy, with adequate energy to meet your daily commitments.

- Engage in good sleep hygiene
- Eat a healthy diet
- Take care of your health and address any physical or medical issues
- Do physical activity every day
- Explore complementary medicine (e.g., traditional medicine, massage therapy, acupuncture, osteopathy, naturopathy)
- Use a weighted blanket

SPIRITUAL

Help you have perspective beyond your daily life.

- Create a gratitude practice (e.g., write down 2 things you are grateful for each day)
- Practice mindfulness (e.g., meditation, mindful movement)
- Engage with a spiritual/religious community
- Connect with a spiritual leader or spiritual care practitioner
- Spend time in nature

MENTAL

Help you think clearly and intellectually engage in the demands of daily life.

- Keep a journal and write regularly
- Practice relaxation
- Engage in a hobby
- Read books that you enjoy
- Learn some time-management strategies
- Challenge your mind (e.g., puzzles, crosswords, memory games)

EMOTIONAL/RELATIONAL

Help you safely experience a wide range of emotions.

- Work on building healthy friendships
- Meet with a therapist whom you trust
- Find someone whom you can talk to about stressors
- Attend a drop-in support group
- Send messages to people who matter to you (without need for response)

BUILD YOUR TOOL BELT: WHAT RESOURCES ARE BEST FOR YOU?

PHYSICAL/SENSORY

SPIRITUAL

MENTAL

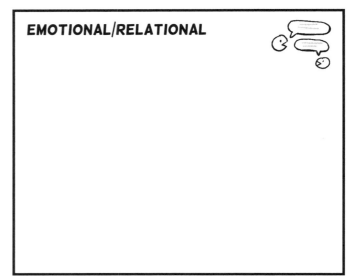

EMOTIONAL/RELATIONAL

TIPS AND TRICKS FOR BUILDING YOUR SELF-CARE TOOL BELT

1. Be patient with the process of identifying self-care tools and activities that you enjoy. This may be a new experience for you if no one has helped you identify these resources before.

2. Try out different ways to resource yourself to see what works best. Talk to other people about what works for them and experiment for yourself.

3. Make a list of resources that work for you and that you are curious to try.

4. After you create a self-care plan, keep this in a place where you can see it every day. Share this with trusted others so that they can help you follow through with your plan.

5. Remember that changes in self-care habits accumulate as you repeat them. The benefits aren't always noticeable at first.

6. Aim for small changes and practice self-care regularly. With practice and self-compassion, these tools will become automatic habits that will offer you a solid foundation for moving through your life.

7. Re-assess how you are doing every 2-3 months. It's important to acknowledge what's working or isn't working for you and change your plan accordingly.

Chapter 3

Complex Posttraumatic Stress Disorder (cPTSD)

Janet Lee-Evoy and Abby Hershler

Background

Posttraumatic stress disorder (PTSD) describes symptoms people may experience after exposure to actual or threatened death, serious injury, or sexual violence. This can include exposure to a natural disaster, a serious accident, a terrorist act, war/combat, or physical and sexual assault. These traumas can be single-incident traumas or complex, prolonged, interpersonal traumas (APA 2013).

There has been debate about whether the type of traumatic exposure (e.g., repeated interpersonal childhood trauma as compared with a single-event trauma in adulthood) has an impact on the kind of posttraumatic symptoms that people exhibit. This debate has given rise to the concept of complex posttraumatic stress disorder (cPTSD), a diagnosis that identifies symptoms experienced by survivors of complex trauma. Complex trauma has been described as repeated or prolonged exposure to traumatic events that are interpersonal and from which escape is difficult, such as childhood abuse, domestic violence, genocide, and institutions of organized violence (Herman 1992).

While the *Diagnostic and Statistical Manual of Mental Disorders*, fifth edition (DSM-5), does not include the diagnosis of cPTSD, it broadens the definition of PTSD found in prior editions. The latest definition includes a new group of symptoms (alterations in cognition and mood) and also subtypes that identify dissociative symptoms. The World Health Organization (WHO) took a different position about the need for a distinct diagnostic category for complex trauma and introduced cPTSD in the eleventh version of its *International Classification of Diseases* (ICD-11) in 2018.

PTSD includes three symptom clusters: re-experiencing the traumatic event in the present; avoiding reminders of the traumatic event; and a sense of current threat (hypervigilance). cPTSD includes these three core symptom clusters as well as three additional clusters: problems with emotion regulation; relational or interpersonal difficulties; and negative self-concept (Herman 1992; WHO 2018).

How to Use This Model

This model can be used to help clients reflect on the ways that past traumatic experiences may continue to affect their mental health and daily functioning and also allow them to reflect on their experiences within the medical system. It may be helpful to review chapter 7, as that chapter provides an explanation for some of the symptoms experienced in cPTSD.

- Start by discussing clients' personal journey to healing and their experience of the medical system and diagnoses. Ask client(s) what experiences have been helpful and unhelpful in their effort to get support. Explore the pros and cons of diagnoses.
- Provide an introduction to the process of evolving diagnoses in the *Diagnostic and Statistical Manual* (DSM) or the World Health Organization's *International Classification of Disease* (ICD). Give examples of how shared understanding of mental illness continues to evolve with research and social change, such as the removal of homosexuality from the DSM in 1973.
- Describe the efforts that clinicians working in childhood trauma have been making to ensure that the impacts of chronic childhood trauma are fully captured in the DSM definition of PTSD, including advocating for the inclusion of cPTSD as a formal diagnosis.
- Note that many people with complex trauma have been labeled with multiple other diagnoses in the past and may find that the diagnosis of cPTSD helps foster a more cohesive understanding of their symptoms.
- Identify the differences and similarities between PTSD and cPTSD, using the model to guide the discussion.
- Explain that each symptom cluster can be used as an entry point to identify pathways for recovery and healing. For example, emotion regulation difficulties can be addressed through self-awareness and skill building, and relational difficulties can be addressed by mindfully engaging in healthier interpersonal experiences (e.g., therapy, safe relationships).

Educational Gems

- Reflect on your own role in the system and acknowledge power differentials. Express your willingness to hear about clients' experiences of encounters with people in your profession or in the healthcare system.
- Acknowledge that diagnosis may be normalizing, resulting in clients feeling less alone. It can also be useful for clarifying symptoms and for documentation and communication to other individuals or organizations.
- However, for some, diagnosis is stigmatizing and reductive, leading to feelings of confusion, rejection, and shame. Identifying these diverse responses to a medical diagnosis may allow for a transparent and helpful discussion.
- The comic can be shared with trusted family members or friends for shared understanding, or with healthcare professionals as a way to self-advocate.
- Acknowledge that seeing these symptoms written down can be overwhelming for some individuals. Use grounding exercises as needed when discussing the model or follow the discussion by identifying options for self-care.

References

American Psychiatric Association (APA). 2013. *Diagnostic and Statistical Manual of Mental Disorders.* 5th ed. Arlington, VA: APA.

Berliner, Lucy, et al. 2018. "ISTSS Guidelines Position Paper on Complex PTSD in Adults." International Society for Traumatic Stress Studies. https://istss.org/getattachment/Treating-Trauma/New-ISTSS-Prevention-and-Treatment-Guidelines/ISTSS_CPTSD-Position-Paper-(Adults)_FNL.pdf.aspx.

Herman, Judith. 1992. "Complex PTSD: A Syndrome in Survivors of Prolonged and Repeated Trauma." *Journal of Traumatic Stress* 5(3): 377–91.

World Health Organization (WHO). 2018. *International Classification of Diseases for Mortality and Morbidity Statistics.* 11th release. https://icd.who.int/browse11/l-m/en.

COMPLEX POSTTRAUMATIC STRESS DISORDER (CPTSD)

JOURNEY TO HEALING

WHERE DO DIAGNOSES COME FROM?

The *Diagnostic and Statistical Manual of Mental Disorders* (DSM) is a book that describes the criteria or symptoms of mental health disorders.

The definitions in the DSM change as our understanding of mental health grows. Currently, there is a debate about the way that PTSD has been described.

Many are advocating for adding cPTSD to the DSM because they feel the current definition does not completely capture the symptoms experienced by survivors of chronic childhood trauma.

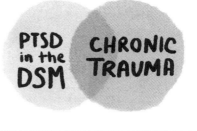

WHAT DOES DIAGNOSIS MEAN TO YOU?
Circle or draw your answers.

Misdiagnosis
Confusing
Stigma
Loss of identity
Rejection
Blame

Freeing
Understanding
Documentation
Empathy
Normalizing
Validation
Clarity

© **2020 Trauma Education Comics, P. Nguyen, L. Hughes and A. Hershler**
References Berliner, Lucy, et al. 2018. "ISTSS Guidelines Position Paper on Complex PTSD in Adults." International Society for Traumatic Stress Studies. https://istss.org/getattachment/Treating-Trauma/New-ISTSS-Prevention-and-Treatment-Guidelines/ISTSS_CPTSD-Position-Paper-(Adults)_FNL.pdf.aspx.
Herman, Judith. 1992. "Complex PTSD: A Syndrome in Survivors of Prolonged and Repeated Trauma." *Journal of Traumatic Stress* 5(3): 377-91.

COMPLEX POSTTRAUMATIC STRESS DISORDER (cPTSD)

(as defined in the World Health Organization's International Classification of Diseases)

cPTSD is a diagnosis that identifies the symptoms experienced by survivors of complex trauma. Complex traumas have been described as repeated or prolonged exposure to traumatic events that are interpersonal and from which escape is difficult, such as childhood abuse.

THERE ARE 6 CLUSTERS OF SYMPTOMS IN cPTSD ...

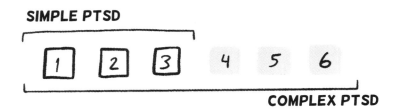

The first three clusters are 3 of the core criteria for the diagnosis of PTSD and cPTSD

1. RE-EXPERIENCING • Unwanted memories • Nightmares • Flashbacks • Emotional distress when reminded of trauma • Physical symptoms when reminded of trauma	**2. AVOIDANCE** • Avoiding thoughts or feelings that are reminders of the trauma • Avoiding people, places, activities, objects that are reminders of the trauma	**3. SENSE OF CURRENT THREAT** • Hypervigilance • Exaggerated startle response • Feeling "on edge"

The next three clusters are an additional 3 core criteria included in the diagnosis of cPTSD

4. PROBLEMS WITH EMOTION REGULATION • Rapid mood changes • Persistent sadness • Suicidal thoughts • Dissociation and emotional numbing • Tension reduction behaviors (e.g., self-harm) • Difficulty experiencing pleasure or positive emotions	**5. RELATIONAL DIFFICULTIES** • Difficulty maintaining long-term relationships • Intense, short-term relationships • Difficulty feeling close to others • Avoidance or disinterest in social connection • Repeated search for a rescuer	**6. NEGATIVE SELF-CONCEPT** • Negative beliefs about your worth and value • Thinking that something is wrong with you • Pervasive feelings of shame or guilt

References Berliner, Lucy, et al. 2018. "ISTSS Guidelines Position Paper on Complex PTSD in Adults." International Society for Traumatic Stress Studies. https://istss.org/getattachment/Treating-Trauma/New-ISTSS-Prevention-and-Treatment-Guidelines/ISTSS_CPTSD-Position-Paper-(Adults)_FNL.pdf.aspx.
Herman, Judith. 1992. "Complex PTSD: A Syndrome in Survivors of Prolonged and Repeated Trauma." *Journal of Traumatic Stress* 5(3): 377-91.

Chapter 4

Window of Tolerance

Abby Hershler

Background

"Window of tolerance" is a term introduced by psychiatrist, educator, and author Dan J. Siegel in 1999. It has evolved as a concept (Ogden, Minton, and Pain 2006) and is now widely used in trauma-focused education to provide a framework for understanding physiological and emotional responses to daily life stressors and reminders of traumatic past experiences.

This model proposes that individuals have an optimal zone of arousal within the window of tolerance where they can manage daily stress and challenges. However, the experience of childhood trauma causes the window of tolerance to narrow. As an individual's reactions to stressors intensify, it becomes more difficult to access strategies and resources to manage distress. This often shows up as overwhelming emotions, unwanted thoughts, uncomfortable sensations, or unhealthy behavioral impulses. This model can be used to help clients mindfully track these states, build resources to tolerate daily stressors, and proactively implement resources to widen their window of tolerance.

It is useful to discuss the window of tolerance model as a foundation at the beginning of

therapy. Clients can be encouraged to reflect regularly on where they locate themselves on the window of tolerance model. When a client recognizes they are outside of their window, they can respond with awareness and practice using resources that help them re-enter or expand their window. Clients can also actively engage in self-care practices to expand their baseline window of tolerance in order to tolerate stressors as they arise.

How to Use This Model

Start by discussing each zone in the window of tolerance model. Ask clients to describe or write down thoughts, feelings, sensations, and behavioral impulses that are indications of being in each zone for themselves.

· Ask client(s) where they usually find themselves in this model. What is their baseline? How do they know this?
· Ask client(s) to notice where they would locate themselves on the model in this moment. What are the thoughts, feelings, sensations, and behavioral impulses that indicate this?
· Brainstorm strategies and resources for expanding the window of tolerance or

returning to the zone of optimal arousal. What strategies are helpful in hyperarousal? What strategies are helpful in hypoarousal?

Optimal Arousal

· In this zone, you are able to integrate information and remain aware of your emotions, thoughts, sensations, and behavioral impulses.
· The goal is to have a wide window of tolerance in order to tolerate stressors and emotions that are inevitable in everyday life.
· Many people who have experienced repeated trauma have a narrow zone of optimal arousal. Sometimes we refer to the narrow width as being "pencil" or "toothpick" thin.

Hyperarousal

· Fight, flight, and freeze are the animal defense system responses that are most common in this zone.

Examples of experiences in this zone:
· Feelings such as anxiety, fear, and anger.
· Physical experiences and sensations such as physical tension, racing heart, and shortness of breath.
· Thoughts such as "Something bad is going to happen to me," "I'm in trouble," or "I have to get out of here."
· Impulses such as the desire to run, fight, or yell.

Hypoarousal

· Collapse and feigned death are the animal defense system responses that are most common in this zone.

Examples of experiences in this zone:
· Feelings such as sadness, loneliness, and shame.
· Physical experiences such as numbness, disconnection, sleepiness, and heavy limbs.
· Thoughts such as "I'm tired," "Something is wrong with me," or "Why bother?"

· Impulses such as the urge to sleep or hide.

Educational Gems

· Chronic states of hyperarousal and hypoarousal are difficult to tolerate. Naturally, the body will seek equilibrium by engaging in tension reduction or survival coping behaviors (e.g., substance use, self-injury, eating, isolation, etc.).
· When the window of tolerance is narrow, clients can easily overshoot the zone of optimal arousal, which results in rapid movement between hyperarousal and hypoarousal.
· Childhood trauma necessitates activation of survival responses, often for prolonged periods of time.
· Acknowledge that being in the window of tolerance can feel unfamiliar or even dangerous.
· Therapy happens on the edges of the window of tolerance. We can help clients widen their window of tolerance by supporting them in gradually tolerating states of discomfort while practicing grounding and resourcing.
· It is important for clients to practice self-resourcing when they are in their window of tolerance. Using emotional regulation skills when they are less distressed will increase the chance that these resources are available during times of stress.
· Remind clients that it takes time and patience for a resource to become a habit.

References

Ogden, Pat, and Kekuni Minton. 2000. "Sensorimotor Psychotherapy: One Method for Processing Traumatic Memory." *Traumatology* 6(3): 149–73.
Ogden, Pat, Kekuni Minton, and Clare Pain. 2006. *Trauma and the Body: A Sensorimotor Approach to Psychotherapy.* New York: W. W. Norton.
Siegel, Daniel J. 1999. *The Developing Mind: Toward a Neurobiology of Interpersonal Experience.* New York: Guilford Press.

WINDOW OF TOLERANCE

This model provides a framework for understanding physical and emotional responses to daily life stressors and reminders of past trauma.

WHAT IS HYPERAROUSAL?

Too much arousal can result in HYPERarousal. You may feel things that make you want to fight or run away.

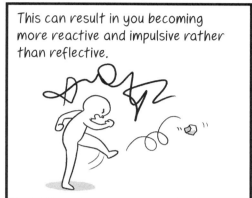

This can result in you becoming more reactive and impulsive rather than reflective.

WHAT IS "BEING IN YOUR WINDOW OF TOLERANCE"?

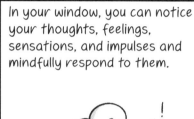

In your window, you can notice your thoughts, feelings, sensations, and impulses and mindfully respond to them.

This is not a stress-free state...

... but rather a state where you can ride the waves of daily stress without becoming overwhelmed.

WHAT IS HYPOAROUSAL?

When there is too little activation, this can result in HYPOarousal. This can cause feelings of extreme fatigue, numbness, and lethargy.

I feel nothing

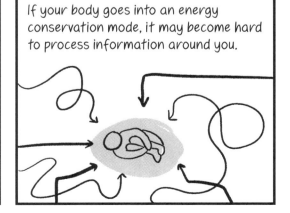

If your body goes into an energy conservation mode, it may become hard to process information around you.

© 2020 Trauma Education Comics, P. Nguyen, L. Hughes and A. Hershler
Adapted from Ogden, Pat, and Kekuni Minton. 2000. "Sensorimotor Psychotherapy: One Method for Processing Traumatic Memory." *Traumatology* 6(3): 149-73.
Siegel, Daniel J. 1999. *The Developing Mind: Toward a Neurobiology of Interpersonal Experience.* New York: Guilford Press.

WINDOW OF TOLERANCE

This model provides a framework for understanding physical and emotional responses to daily life stressors and reminders of past trauma. Draw or write your thoughts, feelings, sensations, and impulses.

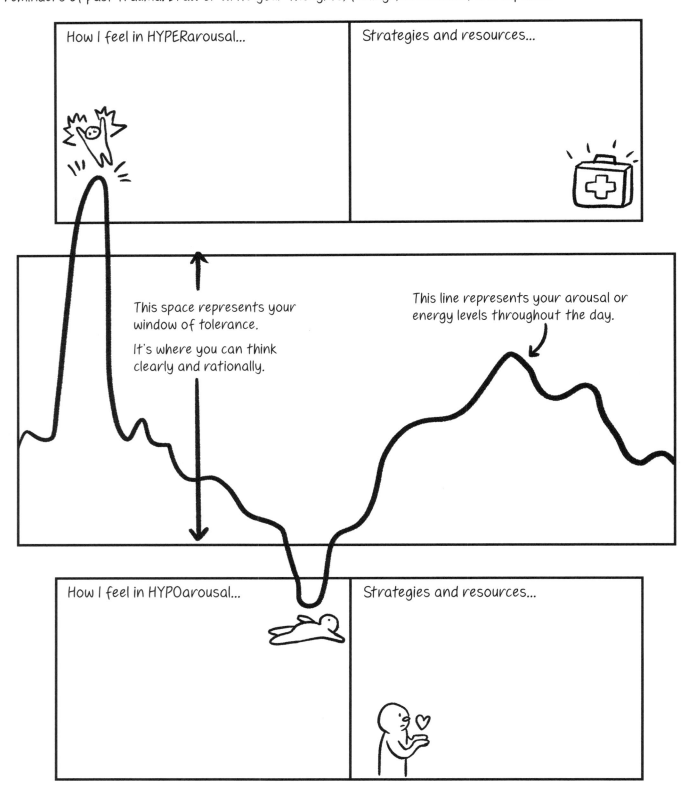

How I feel in HYPERarousal...

Strategies and resources...

This space represents your window of tolerance.

It's where you can think clearly and rationally.

This line represents your arousal or energy levels throughout the day.

How I feel in HYPOarousal...

Strategies and resources...

Adapted from Ogden, Pat, and Kekuni Minton. 2000. "Sensorimotor Psychotherapy: One Method for Processing Traumatic Memory." *Traumatology* 6(3): 149-73.
Siegel, Daniel J. 1999. *The Developing Mind: Toward a Neurobiology of Interpersonal Experience.* New York: Guilford Press.

Chapter 5

The Trigger Scale

Mahum Musheer

Background

In this model, the term "trigger" refers to internal or external reminders of childhood trauma that are encoded in the memory system. When an experience in the present links to an experience from the past, memories can flood into awareness in the form of physical sensations, thoughts, emotions, and/or impulses. Clients describe this experience as a rapid, uncontrolled, and unpredictable movement toward a state of hyperarousal or hypoarousal. This rapid biological response can be experienced as particularly distressing and disempowering for individuals who have limited trust and experience of choice as it relates to their bodies.

The trigger scale model is a framework that encourages clients to slow down and reflect on their individual responses to triggers. In this model, the movement toward hyperarousal or hypoarousal is depicted on a scale of 0 to +/-10. This model encourages clients to notice incremental changes that indicate activation. By noticing and recording what happens somatically, emotionally, cognitively, and behaviorally when triggered, clients can begin to familiarize themselves with these internal cues. This is a starting place to identify early signs of distress and engage in grounding strategies to reduce activation, leading to a greater sense of choice and empowerment in the present.

How to Use This Model

The trigger scale can be used in a group or individual therapy setting to explore signs of low, medium, and high levels of distress. You may also find it helpful to refer to chapter 8 when discussing this model.

- Start by asking the client(s) to reflect on where they would place themselves on their trigger scale in the present moment. Support them to write or draw the somatic, emotional, physical, and behavioral impulses that are specific to that point on their scale.
- Is this your baseline? If not, how would you describe your baseline?
- What thoughts, feelings, physical sensations, or impulses let you know that you are at this point on the scale?

Table 5.1 | Trigger scale levels of distress

Level of distress	Examples
Low (0 to 3 or 0 to -3)	• Physical sensations: shortness of breath or holding their breath, tightness in the chest, numbness • Feelings: anxiety, irritation, hurt • Thoughts: "here we go again," "it's happening again" • Impulses: a desire to hide or leave and get away
Medium (4 to 6 or -4 to -6)	• Physical sensations: increased level of energy/tension or numbness in the body, heavy limbs, fogginess • Feelings: fear, sadness, shame, anger • Thoughts: "this always happens to me," "something is wrong with me," "why bother?" • Impulses: to sleep, run, or yell
High (7 to 10 or -7 to -10)	• Physical sensations: significant energy/tension, uncontainable urgency, total numbness, reduced vision • Feelings: rage, hopelessness, helplessness, worthlessness • Thoughts: "I'm not worth it," "nothing is going to work," "I don't want to live another day like this" • Impulses: to fight, hurt self or others, or collapse

Upward/Downward Spiral

When clients experience high levels of distress, they can shift into an upward or a downward spiral. These states are often experienced as intolerable and unsustainable. There may be an urge to engage in tension-reduction behaviors (e.g., self-harm, substance use, suicidality, disordered eating). When people have limited resources to manage distress that feels overwhelming and all-consuming, it is natural that they will turn to anything that can provide relief. This model offers an opportunity to normalize and destigmatize survival coping behaviors. While these behaviors are designed to reduce tension in the moment, they often result in a secondary emotion of shame, guilt, or regret that adds to the distress and deepens the sense of need. The hope is that, over time, clients will develop other coping and resourcing strategies that will decrease the necessity to turn to survival coping strategies.

· Explore with client(s) the tension-reduction or survival coping behaviors they engage in.

Managing Distress Early and Shifting One's Baseline

When clients are aware of early indicators of distress along the trigger scale, they are more likely to succeed in effectively responding to activation before they have entered the upward or downward spiral.

Additionally, the trigger scale can be used to notice a change in a client's baseline level of distress. When clients check in with themselves regularly, practice grounding skills, and engage in daily self-care, they can shift their baseline over time. The aim is to move incrementally down the trigger scale—closer to "0"—and to take time to recognize and celebrate these changes.

Educational Gems

· Start by asking clients what words, images, and symbols they associate with the term "trigger."
· Triggers are not necessarily overt, identifiable events. They can be conscious or unconscious, internal or external, relational or non-relational (e.g., the weather, holidays).

Connection/disconnection in relationships are also common triggers.

· Consider asking clients to identify some of their triggers without reliving them. When triggers remain unconscious or unnamed, they can feel overwhelming and out of control. It is often normalizing and destigmatizing for clients to identify their triggers.

· "0" on the scale is a state of calm. Many people will say that they have never experienced this state and that their system is always over- or under-activated.

· When exploring "0" with clients who may be unfamiliar with this state, it can be helpful to begin by asking, "What does being okay look like?"

· Clients may find it reassuring to learn that many people identify a baseline that is above or below "0." One goal of therapy is to support clients in shifting their baseline closer to "0."

· Consider completing the trigger scale in a detailed way, in which reactions/responses to triggers are explored at each numerical increment between 0 and 10 or 0 and -10.

· The trigger scale can be tailored for a particular issue (e.g., anger, relationship, work conflict).

· Some clients will find it easier to think about a trigger scale that moves in one direction only and includes *both* states of hyperarousal and hypoarousal at the same time. In this case, encourage clients to draw their own trigger scale.

· It is helpful for some clients to acknowledge that it is common to fluctuate rapidly between hyperarousal and hypoarousal or feel both states at the same time (e.g., "my mind is racing at a 6 but my body is collapsed at a -4").

References

Fisher, Janina. 2017. *Healing the Fragmented Selves of Trauma Survivors: Overcoming Internal Self-Alienation.* New York: Routledge.

Ogden, Pat, Kekuni Minton, and Clare Pain. 2006. *Trauma and the Body: A Neurobiologically Informed Approach to Clinical Practice.* New York: W. W. Norton.

TRIGGER SCALE

A trigger is a present-day reminder of a past trauma. When triggered, your animal defense system kicks in and you can shift into fight/flight/freeze (HYPERarousal) or collapse (HYPOarousal).

This scale is an opportunity to slow down and get to know yourself so that you have more control over how you react in response to being triggered. It may feel like you go from 0 to 10 or –10 very quickly or even that you never started at 0 to begin with.

TRIGGER SCALE REFLECTION AND RESOURCES

What resources help me move closer to a "0" on my scale?

Chapter 6

Parallel Lives

Lesley Hughes

Background

The "parallel lives" model was developed in 2003 by Deirdre Fay, a psychotherapist and educator in the field of trauma. Her visual metaphor represents a way of looking at what happens when people find themselves responding to situations in the present with an intensity fueled by the past. When an individual is triggered, material from the past explodes or implodes into the present in the form of thoughts, feelings, sensations, impulses, or behaviors. When the unfinished piece of history gets activated in the moment, the present reaction becomes a combination of both current and past responses. Someone may not be aware that their reaction is linked to the past at the time it is happening, which can add to distress and confusion. This model provides a framework to help clients identify moments when the past is conflated with the present and develop skills to separate the past from the present in order to make clearer decisions based on current reality and needs.

How to Use This Model

This model can be used in a group or individual therapy setting to explore present-day situations that elicit strong reactions. When the intensity of a reaction is disproportionate to the current situation, this is often a clue that there is a link to the past. The aim is to support clients in gaining psychological distance between past events and events in the present in order to identify triggering experiences and respond more flexibly to these experiences over time. You may also find it helpful to refer to chapter 5 when discussing this model.

Part 1: Here and Now

Start by noting the line that distinguishes the "here and now" from the "there and then." Ask client(s) to write down indications of the "here and now" for themselves.

How do you know you are in the "here and now"?
· Clear thinking.
· Realistic about safety.
· Present focus.

- Able to adapt and be flexible.
- Aware of feelings, thoughts, and sensations.
- Can connect to self inside and out.
- "Okay" if things change.

Something Happens

An event in the "here and now" occurs. For example, you have an argument with a friend, your heart starts racing, there is an upcoming anniversary of an abuser's death, your child turns the age you were when the abuse started, or someone stands too close to you on the bus. It is important to emphasize that "something actually happens," as it can be useful to return to this event later in the model. The thing that happens "trips up" the individual, and the line between "here and now" and "there and then" gets crossed. When the line between "here and now" and "there and then" gets crossed, the individual gets tangled up in the thoughts, feelings, sensations, impulses, and behaviors associated with the past event. It can be hard to know that the present moment is being fueled by the past when it is happening now.

Part 2: There and Then

Ask client(s) to write down indications of the "there and then" for themselves.

How do you know you are in the "there and then"?

- Foggy thinking.
- Rigid ideas about right and wrong.
- Feeling physically paralyzed.
- Feeling overwhelmed.
- Physical or emotional exhaustion.
- All-or-nothing thinking.
- Disconnected from feelings, thoughts, and sensations.

- Feeling detached from oneself or others.

Ask client(s) if they have a recent example they'd like to share.

- What situations tend to activate the past exploding into the present?

Part 3: Separating the "Here and Now" from the "There and Then"

Ask client(s) to notice the thoughts, feelings, and sensations as cues that they may be experiencing a reaction in the present moment that is fueled by the past.

- Does this remind you of someone or something about yourself?
- Is this event reminiscent of your past experiences?
- Slow down any sense of urgency with soothing statements (e.g., "I am not in immediate danger," "I can take good care of myself," "This is not an emergency").
- Is there someone you can reach out to for support?

After returning to the present, encourage clients to reflect on their needs.

- Do you need to revisit the "something that happened" (i.e., the triggering event)?
- Is there something you can do to take care of yourself?
- Can you identify and express your needs directly (e.g., "I need some time to calm down before I continue this conversation")?
- Can you set a boundary (e.g., "Can you please move over a little? Your elbow is pushing into my back," "I need to take a walk")?
- Practice self-compassion (e.g., "This is hard and painful and it's okay to feel sad and to cry").
- Get help from a friend, a therapist, a healthcare provider, or a support group.

It is important to seek relational repair once the intensity from the past has settled. When a reaction is fueled by the past, expressions of affect and behaviors are often disproportionate to the situation. In relationships, dysregulated expression is likely to be met with defensiveness or equal intensity, resulting in relationship rupture. This contributes to a vicious cycle of distress and unmet needs, replicating the dynamics of the original trauma.

Educational Gems

· Remind clients that the aim is to remain in the present moment even as they are feeling pulled to the past (e.g., "can you keep one foot in the present, one foot in the past?").
· Acknowledge that cultivating new habits and patterns is difficult work.
· Survival responses are often a clue that reminders from the past are being re-activated in the present. Clients will often describe themselves as "existing" but not "living."

· Identify and normalize that even good feelings can feel uncomfortable (e.g., pleasure) and trigger responses from the past. Identifying and normalizing this can be useful in the context of childhood trauma.
· Support individuals in using this model to identify patterns and triggers. Acknowledge and appreciate that there may be protective parts or aspects of self that do not fully recognize ways these patterns have outgrown their utility in the present.

References

Fay, Deirdre. 2020. *Becoming Safely Embodied: Step by Step Guide to Organize the Disorganized Inner World*. New York: Morgan James.

PARALLEL LIVES

HERE AND NOW

THERE AND THEN

Adapted from Fay, Deirdre. 2020. *Becoming Safely Embodied: Step by Step Guide to Organize the Disorganized Inner World.* New York: Morgan James.

PARALLEL LIVES

Write or draw strategies in this space that help you stay in the HERE and NOW.

WHAT CAN I DO NOW?

Adapted from Fay, Deirdre. 2020. *Becoming Safely Embodied: Step by Step Guide to Organize the Disorganized Inner World.* New York: Morgan James.

Chapter 7

The Brain—Three Parts

Susshma Persaud

Background

Physician and neuroscientist Paul D. MacLean introduced the triune brain theory, suggesting that the human brain is three brains functioning as one. These "three brains" include the brainstem (reptilian brain), the limbic system (mammalian brain), and the prefrontal cortex (human brain) (MacLean 1990). Although it is widely understood that this model is a simplification of brain function, it continues to be a helpful framework in trauma therapy.

By exploring the actions and interactions of these parts of the brain, this model helps clients understand how they become emotionally "hijacked" by reminders of past trauma, and it provides a framework to help them identify healthy resources for managing these emotional responses.

How to Use This Model

Start by explaining the goals of this model, including:

- To recognize the difference between real and imagined threats.

- To shift well-worn (but no longer helpful) behavioral and emotional responses to reminders of past trauma.
- To develop resources to self-regulate in response to perceived dangers.

Use the comic on the first page to explain that there are two pathways through the brain for responding to sensory information:

- The fast pathway, which engages the animal defense responses, allows you to react quickly to perceived danger.
- The slow pathway allows for a more mindful response to perceived threats.

Explain that you will be discussing the three parts of the brain and each of their roles in processing information.

Consider drawing a simplified representation of the brain as a large oval divided into three parts, each representing one part of the brain. You can also draw a shape in the mammalian brain to represent the amygdala.

Discuss each part of the brain as described below.

Reptilian Brain (Brainstem)

- Connects the brain to the spinal cord.
- Originates in the lowest, most primitive part of the brain.
- Is responsible for basic functions needed to preserve life, such as digestion, breathing, and heart rate.
- Is important for automatic responses, such as jumping back from the edge of the road when a car drives too close to you.
- Uses the animal defense responses (attach cry, fight, flight, freeze, collapse) to maintain safety.

Mammalian Brain (Limbic System)

- Is the emotion and memory center of the brain.
- Holds gut memories, emotional blueprints, traumatic memories, and non-verbal emotions.
- Has a limited concept of time, which explains why many traumatized clients feel stuck in the past.
- Contains the amygdala, which is referred to as the "smoke detector" of the brain. The amygdala is always on alert for threat or danger.
- Survivors of childhood trauma have a highly attuned amygdala that is hypersensitive to danger. The alarm will ring at the smallest indication of threat, including present-day reminders of the past trauma.
- The pathways from the mammalian brain to the reptilian brain are known as the primal pathways or "low road." These pathways provide a fast but inexact response to perceived dangers.

Human Brain (Prefrontal Cortex)

- Is responsible for executive function and regulating the nervous system.
- Helps with regulating emotion and tolerating distress.
- Is very small at birth and starts developing in the toddler years. Development is optimized with support and guidance from care providers and teachers.
- The pathways between the mammalian brain and the human brain are slower but more precise. They are called the "high road."
- Without help to build the slower pathways between the prefrontal cortex and the limbic system/amygdala, most people will use the fast or primal pathway to respond to perceived dangers and threats.
- The prefrontal cortex can be broken down into three sections: working memory, the noticing pathway, and the soothing pathway.
- Working memory is the part of the brain responsible for higher executive functioning (e.g., insight, problem-solving, and drawing conclusions). The working memory does not have direct access to the amygdala when the limbic system is activated.
- Use the second page of the comic to help explain that you cannot activate the "thinking" parts of the brain to solve problems when in immediate distress.
- Explain that there are other pathways that can help you respond to distress and manage big emotions in response to traumatic triggers. These are the noticing and soothing pathways of the brain. Unlike the working memory, they do have direct access to the amygdala.
- Explain that when you consciously tune into resources that activate the noticing and

soothing pathways of the brain, you can soothe and regulate the body. This results in a sense of somatic (embodied) safety and allows the working memory to come back online.

Invite your client(s) to brainstorm their ideas around the role of each part of the human brain and to name noticing and soothing resources that they find helpful.

Educational Gems

· From an evolutionary perspective, our brains have been hardwired for survival. The brain's main concern is with keeping us alive when there is an imminent threat. This model can help clients decrease self-blame and shame and normalize their survival reactions to past trauma.
· The brain also has a negativity bias built into it. This makes negative experiences seem more significant than positive ones (Baumeister et al. 2001).
· The brain has the ability to change continuously throughout an individual's life. It therefore has the ability to heal itself with the conscious practice of strategies in a paced way (Doidge 2005).
· The creation of new neural pathways takes time. This practice requires stepping out of your comfort zone, making behavioral changes, and being patient and kind with yourself.
· Developing the soothing and noticing pathways expands opportunities for health and well-being (e.g., mindfully noticing instead of dissociating).
· The noticing and soothing pathways in the brain are responsible for mindful observation, fostering curiosity and non-judgment toward thoughts, feelings, and sensations (Fisher 2011).

References

Baumeister, Roy F., Ellen Bratslavsky, Catrin Finkenauer, and Kathleen D. Vohs. 2001. "Bad Is Stronger than Good." *Review of General Psychology* 5(4): 323–70.

Doidge, Norman. 2005. *The Brain That Changes Itself: Stories of Personal Triumph from the Frontiers of Brain Science.* New York: Penguin Books.

Fisher, Janina. 2011. *Psychoeducational Aids for Working with Psychological Trauma.* Boston: Center for Integrative Healing.

MacLean, Paul D. 1990. *The Triune Brain in Evolution: Role in Paleocerebral Functions.* New York: Plenum Press.

Siegel, Daniel J. 2017. "Hand Model of the Brain" (video). August 9, 2017. https://www.youtube.com/watch?v=f-m2YcdMdFw.

van der Kolk, Bessel A. 2014. *The Body Keeps the Score: Brain, Mind and Body in the Healing of Trauma.* New York: Penguin Books.

THE BRAIN - THREE PARTS

In this model, the brain is divided into three parts with distinct functions that enable us to respond to danger in the world.

HOW DOES THE BRAIN RESPOND TO DANGER?

The brain constantly receives and processes information. It has two pathways for processing this information.

The FAST pathway is the animal defense pathway. This is designed to keep us safe.

The SLOW pathway is used when we are able to regulate our emotions, stay grounded and take time to think.

oh, it's just a stick

When you have experienced childhood trauma, the brain is accustomed to responding to danger and...

... the fast pathway becomes very well traveled.

RING!!

As an adult, it is important to mindfully build the slower pathway.

THE THREE PARTS OF THE BRAIN

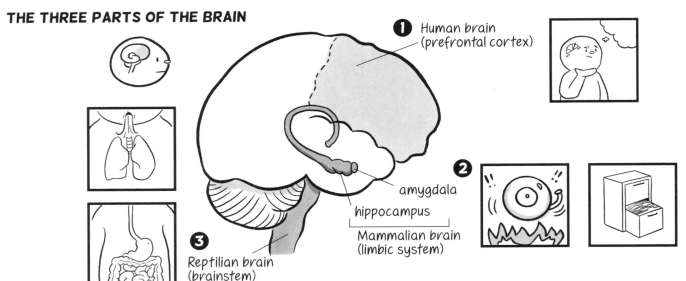

❶ Human brain (prefrontal cortex)

amygdala

hippocampus

❷ Mammalian brain (limbic system)

❸ Reptilian brain (brainstem)

© 2020 Trauma Education Comics, P. Nguyen, L. Hughes and A. Hershler
Adapted from MacLean, Paul D. 1990. *The Triune Brain in Evolution: Role in Paleocerebral Functions.* New York: Plenum Press.

WHAT CAN WE DO TO BUILD A SLOWER PATHWAY?

Trauma survivors have a highly attuned amygdala or "smoke alarm" that responds to even the smallest sign of danger. In this model, there are three ways to use the human brain to regulate the amygdala, but only two of them are available when you are in distress and the smoke alarm is ringing.

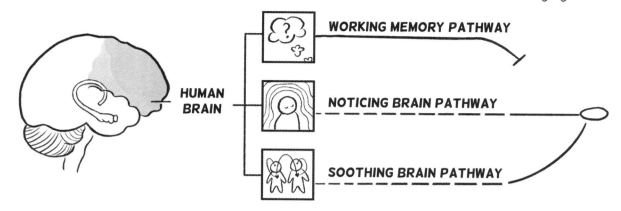

WORKING MEMORY AND TRAUMA

The working memory relies on reasoning, logic and learning to guide decision-making. Humans commonly use working memory to calm their minds and bodies. But as it turns out...

Working memory doesn't directly regulate the amygdala in times of distress.

not connected!

AMYGDALA

That's why you can't "think" your way out of stressful situations.

Working memory can be useful after the stressor has passed in order to process the event.

SOOTHING AND NOTICING PATHWAYS

These pathways are designed to support mindful awareness in the present moment.

The soothing and noticing pathways have direct connections to the amygdala in the mammalian brain.

The noticing brain uses internal or external cues, such as your breath or a warm sensation on your skin, to calm the amygdala and self-regulate.

The soothing brain uses internal and external cues, such as self-compassion or connection with pets or friends, to calm the amygdala and self-regulate.

© 2020 Trauma Education Comics, P. Nguyen, L. Hughes and A. Hershler
Adapted from MacLean, Paul D. 1990. *The Triune Brain in Evolution: Role in Paleocerebral Functions.* New York: Plenum Press.

Chapter 8

How Trauma Impacts Memory

Eva-Marie Stern

Background

Memory is often a distressing topic for clients in first-stage trauma therapy. This model focuses on a practical approach to the subject: the relationship between memory and triggers. Exploring triggers in first-stage trauma therapy is essential in helping clients gain confidence that they can face their day-to-day fears safely.

Experiences are encoded (remembered) in two ways: implicit and explicit.

Implicit memory:
- Is often imprinted as physical sensations or feeling states.
- Lacks clarity, logic, and consists in sensory fragments (e.g., smells, sounds).
- Has little verbal or narrative content.
- Does not shift in intensity over time.

Explicit memory:
- Can be recalled at will (active recall).
- Has a coherent beginning, middle, and end.
- Evolves and changes in intensity over time.

Triggers are a short circuit to past traumatic experiences that have been encoded by implicit memory. Because survivors feel triggered by things that seem neutral to others, they often feel damaged or over-sensitive, confused, angry, "re-traumatized," and ultimately paralyzed. For self-protection, they often avoid situations that evoke triggers and can end up isolated and unable to participate in life, existing rather than living.

Understanding how triggers relate to implicit and explicit memory can be profoundly freeing. The comics offer a framework for discussion by providing the following areas to explore with your client(s):
- Understanding the differences between non-traumatic and trauma-related memory systems.
- Recognizing patterns of avoidance.
- Acknowledging distress in the present.
- Grounding to re-establish safety.
- Processing triggers with a trusted person to help resolve and heal implicit memory fragments.

Explicit memory is like a filing cabinet that has file folders in alphabetical order, and the files inside have dates and page numbers and are kept well organized. It is easy to find what you are looking for and to understand what is written there. You do not worry about finding information when you need it, and it is easy to share it with others if you want to. It is reassuring and makes you feel competent. Implicit memory is like a filing cabinet that does not have folders, and there are no labels, only scraps of torn paper thrown there in a hurry, randomly stuck to each other. It can make you feel embarrassed or ashamed to be asked to find any information in it.

Explicit memory is like looking into a room in daylight: you can look around with confidence and see how one object or piece of furniture is arranged next to another. You can see how big the room is and what color the walls are and describe it to someone else. Implicit memory is like looking into a room through a keyhole or with a flashlight in the dark: you cannot see the whole room, just one disconnected part at a time, and it is hard to describe the room to anyone else.

How to Use This Model

Start by reassuring clients that we will not talk about specific traumatic memories. Instead, we will talk about why triggers come up and what to do about them. To understand triggers, we will start by looking at two ways all experiences are remembered: explicitly and implicitly.

Ask a client or group member to describe a positive personal memory.

· Ask others to pay attention to how the teller is telling her story. Notice how the teller can remember this story at will, recall sensory details, and provide listeners with a clear story that is easy to follow.

· Explain that this is explicit memory.
· Ask the client or group member to brainstorm other neutral examples of explicit memory (e.g., what I had for breakfast, my address and phone number, the last time I went to the store for groceries, etc.).

Now explain that implicit memory is different.
· Ask whether individual clients can play a musical instrument, or ride a bike, or type quickly.
· Can they easily explain to others how to do these things?
· Explain that implicit memory helps us learn complex tasks and perform them without having to remember how to do it in words. This saves us time and energy.
· Explain that implicit memory also protects us by encoding overwhelming experiences and hiding them from our everyday awareness.

Review the comic with your client or group, stopping to discuss questions and comments that arise. You can generate discussion by asking:
· What are the signs that you have been triggered?
· What are the ways that you try to avoid being triggered?
· What strategies do you use to help you recover after being triggered?

Educational Gems
· It is not necessary to remember or work on retrieving memories in order to recover from trauma.
· Pacing is very important. Discuss one trigger at a time, so clients can keep a foot in the present while putting a toe in the past.
· There's no right or wrong way to remember the past. There's a natural range: on one end of the continuum, some people seem to

remember every last detail, and on the other end, others have only a vague sense of what happened.

- Our bodies hold memories of our past experiences, especially when we were overwhelmed or did not have the language to explain these experiences to ourselves at the time. These memories return as "body memories" or triggers when we are adults.
- When traumatic experiences occur before an individual has the language to describe the experience (e.g., preverbal), these will be remembered by the body as "body memories."
- It is normal and healthy to have implicit memory. Notice and appreciate the protective function of the implicit memory system.
- Avoiding triggers is natural for self-protection but can contribute to symptoms of fear and anxiety over time.
- Medical, educational, and justice systems value explicit memories. Understanding implicit memory and the ways that trauma interferes with coding explicit memory can help explain difficulties with learning in a classroom setting as well as struggles with providing a linear and detailed story in a courtroom or medical office.

- Even though we are not asking people to discuss traumatic memories, this topic can evoke triggered memories. As a clinician, you should be attuned to signs of activation throughout the session.
- Clients report distress in not being able to differentiate body sensations from the past and in the present when they arise as triggers. Identifying these triggers as parts/aspects of self that are holding experiences from the past can be helpful in beginning to separate the two experiences.
- Other strategies to use in response to an implicit memory can be found in chapter 2.

References

Levine, Peter. 2015. *Trauma and Memory: Brain and Body in a Search for the Living Past.* Berkeley, CA: North Atlantic Books.

Siegel, Daniel J. 2012. *Pocket Guide to Interpersonal Neurobiology: An Integrative Handbook of the Mind.* New York: W. W. Norton.

van der Kolk, Bessel A. 2014. *The Body Keeps the Score: Brain, Mind, and Body in the Healing of Trauma.* New York: Penguin Books.

HOW TRAUMA IMPACTS MEMORY

Explicit or narrative memory is your active memory. You know what you're remembering.

Implicit memory or procedural memory can be thought of as your "gut memory," where you don't know what or why you're remembering but you have a bodily experience or feeling.

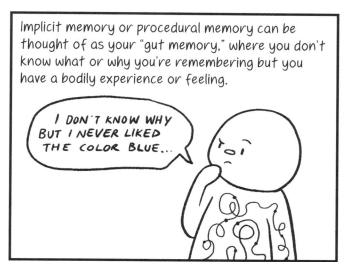

TRAUMA CAN ALTER THE WAY THE BRAIN ENCODES MEMORY.

During overwhelming experiences, trauma is often coded into implicit memory rather than explicit and is recalled through feelings, behaviors, and sensations.

During stressful situations, the body releases hormones that block explicit memory and enhance implicit memory.

Explicit memory is not yet fully formed in childhood.

During a traumatic experience, our attention may be focused on a specific detail instead of the main event.

After a traumatic experience, there is a natural tendency to avoid thoughts, feelings, and remembering of the event.

© 2020 Trauma Education Comics, P. Nguyen, L. Hughes and A. Hershler
Adapted from van der Kolk, B. A. 2014. "Uncovering Secrets." In *The Body Keeps the Score: Brain, Mind, and Body in the Healing of Trauma.* New York: Viking.

WHAT FACTORS CONTRIBUTE TO MEMORY BEING CODED IMPLICITLY?

HOW CAN WE WORK WITH IMPLICIT MEMORY THAT INTRUDES INTO DAILY LIFE?

The first step in addressing implicit memory is to recognize and acknowledge that the past has intruded into the present.

Then, focus on safety and stabilization by using grounding strategies to stay present.

Take notice of positive or neutral objects around you to help you move from the past to the present.

When you feel grounded and present, you can share your feelings and thoughts related to past trauma with a therapist or a trusted friend.

WHAT OTHER STRATEGIES DO YOU USE?

Adapted from van der Kolk, B. A. 2014. "Uncovering Secrets." In *The Body Keeps the Score: Brain, Mind, and Body in the Healing of Trauma.* New York: Viking.

Chapter 9

Structural Dissociation

Holly Miles and Nancy McCallum

Background

"Dissociation" is a term that is widely used to describe a variety of concepts and processes in the human psyche that involve disconnection or fragmentation of individuals' experiences of themselves and the world. The structural dissociation model, introduced by van der Hart, Nijenhuis, and Steele (2006) and built upon by Janina Fisher (2017), provides a framework that views dissociation as widened divisions between parts of self. In this framework, dissociation results from the need to engage simultaneously in the tasks of managing daily living and surviving under threat for extended periods of time.

This comic illustrates how survivors of trauma continue with ordinary activities of daily life (relating to others, exploring their world) at the same time as survival systems are being activated (attach cry, fight, flight, freeze, feigned death). This is particularly common when traumatic experiences have involved caregivers or attachment figures. Dissociation allows these incompatible ways of being to be held by separate parts of the self.

This model can be used to help clients examine how their "here and now" responses to triggers are self-protective patterns. It can also help them understand ways that they may experience variations in their sense of self, understand their capacities and emotional states as adaptations, and, ideally, reduce shame and build more self-compassion. It can be a guide for clients to build awareness of inner states and relationships between parts.

How to Use This Model

This model can be used as a framework for a group therapy session or introduced to clients in individual therapy. The aim is to help clients build awareness, curiosity, and compassion toward their own inner experiences and shift behaviors that are no longer serving them.

Start by defining/describing the "self":
· For the purpose of this model, it can be useful to think of "self" as a core of our being, always present and whole, capable of wisdom and compassion and of witnessing our own experience.

- The self has the capacity to use knowledge and experience to take care of younger, more traumatized parts.
- As we take care of the traumatized parts of ourselves, this self can have a greater presence in our lives.

Define/describe dissociation:
- This term refers to experiences of disconnection between aspects or parts of self, or disconnection of self from the world—that is, knowledge, memories, emotions, and sensations can be held by one part of self and kept distant from, or unknown to, other parts.
- Dissociation is a normal human capacity that everyone experiences sometimes. It is commonplace for people to describe experiences as "I wasn't myself," or "that wasn't like me at all."
- Trauma can lead to more extreme or persistent experiences of dissociation that may become problematic or disruptive.

Discuss how "going on with daily life" parts show up:
- Engaging in skills and capacities for daily living (e.g., school or work tasks, getting along with people, caregiving).
- Experiencing trouble accessing emotions or being vulnerable.
- Having limited knowledge of, or access to, memory of trauma.

Describe how trauma leads to structural dissociation:
- When trauma happens, overwhelming emotions (e.g., fear, rage, hopelessness) and survival responses are activated.
- With recurring or ongoing trauma, the person may need to manage these extreme feelings while also going about the business of everyday life (e.g., daily tasks, school or work, relationships).
- It is difficult to manage both at the same time, so the self "splits" into a part that holds the trauma-related feelings and responses to keep them separate from a part that goes about meeting the needs and expectations of everyday life.
- Traumatic dissociation is an unconscious process; it happens outside of awareness, not by choice or on purpose.

Describe survival strategies used by traumatized parts:
- Our nervous system responds to a sense of danger or threat by activating basic animal defenses for self-protection—attach, fight, flight, freeze, or submit.
- In traumatic situations, especially for children, these animal defenses are essential for survival.
- When traumatized parts are reminded of experiences of trauma, danger, or threat, they may react with these animal defenses in everyday life situations that are uncomfortable or distressing but not dangerous. This can cause problems in adult functioning and relationships. See chapter 7 for more information.

Review the survival strategies listed under each animal defense (fight, flight, freeze, submit, attach) on the illustrated model.
- Ask your client(s) to identify which patterns are most familiar to them.
- Acknowledge that this list contains only examples and may need to be edited by each individual so that the list fits more accurately for them.
- Encourage them to write or draw their answers in the space provided.

Offer validation and understanding, and encourage self-compassion:

- Ask if clients relate to having different parts or aspects of themselves, and how they experience these parts.
- Invite curiosity and self-compassion toward all parts.
- Emphasize that there are no bad parts; all parts come to help.

Acknowledge that there may have been significant relational or attachment difficulties in the past, and that it is understandable that some parts may be afraid, while other parts may be desperate for connection.

- Explore internal relationships between parts by inviting clients to look at their parts through the eyes of their wise adult self.
- Encourage the wise adult self to get to know parts—what their characteristics are, how old they feel, what triggers bring them out, what their roles are, what their worries are, and what their unmet needs are.
- Ask how the client feels toward their parts, and how parts feel toward each other.

Identify ways that these patterns and parts may have been necessary or adaptive at one time but may not be working in current circumstances.

- Identify where parts may have similar hopes or goals (e.g., to be safe, to be loved or cared for).
- Look for opportunities for parts to negotiate conflicts between them and have more compassion and harmony with one another.

Identify coping strategies:

- By getting to know the traumatized parts, the adult self may be able to learn more about their needs and goals—for example, a part may need to have their experience witnessed and

acknowledged, to have bodily needs or self-care tended to, to know that they are safer in the present, to be able to assert boundaries, or to receive relational comfort in response to grief.

- The adult self may be able to meet these needs or get them met in safe and healthy ways so that parts no longer need to engage in their old animal defense–based responses.
- When these parts feel safe, heard, and no longer take over, the self can decide how to navigate everyday life and relationships using their adult knowledge and wisdom.

Educational Gems

- Individuals may or may not identify with the experience of having "parts." Acknowledge diverse ways that people organize and understand their sense of self.
- Emphasize the resilience of having adapted and survived difficult circumstances.
- Normalize regret and other difficult emotions such as guilt, shame, and anger related to how they have coped in the past. These feelings are painful and understandably lead to avoidance of getting to know parts of self. Approach this with understanding.
- Some parts might feel anger or fear toward other parts that have engaged in behaviors that are dangerous or harmful to self or other. These parts can also be seen as trying to help/soothe/protect in the best ways they could at the time they took on that role.
- Discuss with clients whether there are drawbacks to these survival strategies in their current lives.
- Explore mixed or conflicting emotional states using parts language. For example, you may feel angry toward a self-destructive part even while you see it as trying to help, soothe, and protect.

- Certain parts may be less motivated than others to engage in psychotherapy; this may manifest in apparent disengagement, resistance, lateness, or distraction/disruption. These behaviors can also be seen as parts trying to protect, and they should be offered understanding and compassion.
- Individuals often have mixed feelings about the description and examples offered in the attach part.
- If there are parts and patterns that feel stuck in the past, ask if the adult self is able to show the part a picture of something safe or comforting from their life in the present (Fisher, 2017).

References

Fisher, Janina. 2017. *Healing the Fragmented Selves of Trauma Survivors: Overcoming Internal Self-Alienation*. New York: Routledge.

van der Hart, Onno, E. R. S. Nijenhuis, and Kathy Steele. 2006. *The Haunted Self: Structural Dissociation and the Treatment of Chronic Traumatization*. New York: W. W. Norton.

STRUCTURAL DISSOCIATION

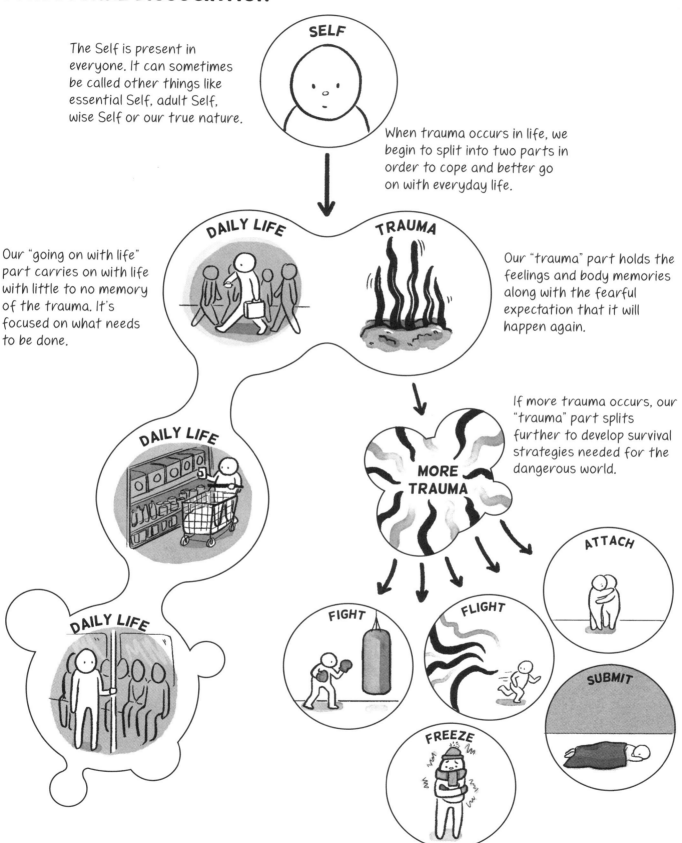

SELF

The Self is present in everyone. It can sometimes be called other things like essential Self, adult Self, wise Self or our true nature.

When trauma occurs in life, we begin to split into two parts in order to cope and better go on with everyday life.

DAILY LIFE

TRAUMA

Our "going on with life" part carries on with life with little to no memory of the trauma. It's focused on what needs to be done.

Our "trauma" part holds the feelings and body memories along with the fearful expectation that it will happen again.

DAILY LIFE

MORE TRAUMA

If more trauma occurs, our "trauma" part splits further to develop survival strategies needed for the dangerous world.

DAILY LIFE

FIGHT

FLIGHT

ATTACH

FREEZE

SUBMIT

Adapted from Fisher, Janina. 2011. *Psychoeducational Aids for Working with Psychological Trauma*. Boston: Center for Integrative Healing.

SURVIVAL STRATEGIES

What coping patterns or parts can you relate to?

FIGHT	FLIGHT	FREEZE	SUBMIT	ATTACH
Angry	Anxious	Afraid	Ashamed	Preoccupied
Suspicious	Distractable	Phobic	Depressed	Wants someone to depend on
Paranoid	Avoidant	Panicky	Passive	Overwhelmed
Suicidal	Trapped	Frozen	Self-loathing	Desperately seeking connection
Judgmental	Ambivalent	Terrified	Collapsed	Need to be rescued
Impulsive	Disordered eating	Wary	Hopeless	Impulse to give care
Mistrustful	Substance use	Agoraphobic	Helpless	

MY "GOING ON WITH LIFE" PARTS
Draw or write your answers.

MY COPING PATTERNS OR PARTS
Draw or write your answers.

WAYS I NOTICE MY PATTERNS AND HELP MY PARTS
Draw or write your answers.

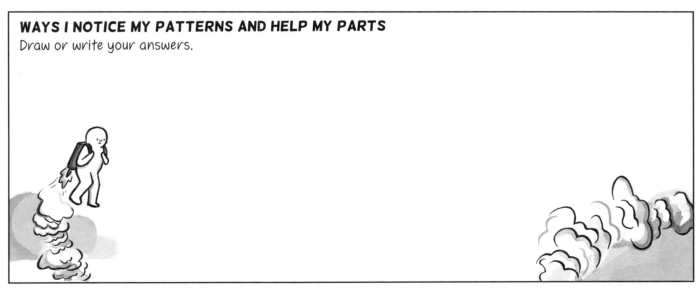

© 2020 Trauma Education Comics, P. Nguyen, L. Hughes and A. Hershler
Adapted from Fisher, Janina. 2011. *Psychoeducational Aids for Working with Psychological Trauma*. Boston: Center for Integrative Healing.

Chapter 10

Karpman's Triangle

Lesley Hughes

Background

Stephen Karpman originally depicted the drama triangle in 1968 as a model of human interactions. As a psychiatrist with an interest in performance and theater, he identified three roles involved in any good drama that repeatedly play out in human relationships. This model allows us to explore ways we get caught in the triangle in the present, repeating patterns unconsciously linked to the past.

Karpman's triangle is used to help clients gain awareness of their patterns of interaction with themselves and others. This is particularly relevant for clients with childhood trauma, because abusive and neglectful relational experiences become the foundation for future relationships. This model helps clients identify unhealthy patterns, explore the unmet needs that drive these patterns, and identify ways to get out of the triangle through awareness and counteraction.

How to Use This Model

This model can be discussed at any point in individual, group, or couples therapy. It is particularly useful when clients are describing an example of a relationship dynamic or stressor in their lives, or when these dynamics are playing out in the therapy setting.

Start by explaining that this model offers a framework for understanding ways we all get caught in relationship roles that often lead to unstable and unsatisfactory relationships. Go on to discuss ways to break out of these patterns.

Step 1: Understanding the Roles

Start with one position on the triangle and brainstorm (see sample in table 10.1 below).

· What are the synonyms, qualities, and traits you associate with each position?
· What are the possible unmet needs or unconscious drives of the person in this position?

Ask your client(s) to reflect, using one or more of the following questions:

· Are there similarities and differences among roles?
· Can you identify your primary pattern/familiar role(s)?

Table 10.1 | Role examples

Role	Synonyms	Qualities/traits	Possible unmet/unconscious needs
Perpetrator	Abuser Bully Aggressor Oppressor	Dominant Intimidating Controlling Demanding Intrusive	To feel in control To feel powerful To gain recognition To avoid vulnerability
Rescuer	Caregiver Savior Helper	Protective Controlling Helpful Martyr	To feel important To be valued To avoid vulnerability
Victim	Sufferer Target Scapegoat	Hopeless Helpless Overwhelmed Vulnerable Scared Weak Dismissed	To receive care and connection To be rescued To avoid responsibility
Neglectful bystander	Neglecter Ignorer Silent witness	Avoidant Denial Dismissive Withholding Inattentive	To stay safe through inaction To avoid vulnerability To avoid and disengage

- Which role is least familiar/comfortable?
- Do you have a recent example you would like to share?
- Is there an experience in therapy or in your daily life that we can discuss using this model?

Step 2: Stepping "Out of the Triangle"
Recognizing these patterns is an important first step toward change. The second part involves making behavioral changes to step out of these roles on the triangle.

Perpetrator role: Empathize and mentalize
- Try to understand the other person's perspective.

Rescuer role: Watch and wait
- Notice any urgency, and wait before stepping in to help someone.

- Allow others to take care of themselves or ask what kind of help they need.
- Tune into your feelings and needs in order to avoid burnout.

Victim role: Act and do
- The aim is to regain a sense of personal empowerment.
- Notice if there are ways to express yourself or to mobilize energy to take action (e.g., setting limits).
- Remind yourself of tools and resources that have helped you cope in the past, and reach out for support if needed.

Neglectful bystander: Mindful observer
- Notice the pattern and re-engage in the present.
- Discuss the dynamic with the survivor and make responsive choices.

- Consider your own feelings and fears.

Educational Gems

- Emphasize that the model is referring to roles, not people (i.e., states, not traits).
- Use everyday, non-traumatic examples to illustrate this model.
- Each of the positions on the triangle can cause pain, come from denied pain, evoke shame, and be associated with a loss of personal power.
- The top of the triangle depicts the two positions that occupy a one-up approach to power: perpetrator and rescuer. The point at the bottom represents a one-down approach to power: victim.
- Consider starting a brainstorm exercise with the rescuer position. This position tends to be relatable for clients and can evoke less shame. Drawbacks of this relational role include burnout, requiring someone be relegated to a victim role, and avoiding one's own needs and problems by focusing on someone else's.
- All of the roles on the triangle are exhausting and uncomfortable. It is not uncommon to move through each of these roles quickly, sometimes in a matter of minutes. An individual can go from feeling hurt that they weren't acknowledged by a colleague (victim role), to withdrawing or not responding (perpetrator role), and later offering a favor to the person (rescuer role).
- Individuals might relate to one of the positions primarily. This situation can be explored as related to one's family of origin and the most useful pattern for surviving childhood. You can offer the following metaphor: Consider this as an eyeglass prescription, written by your early experiences, which shapes the lens through which you view experiences in the present.
- Karpman's triangle can play out in relationship with self. The inner critic or other tension reduction behaviors (e.g., self-injury) are poignant examples of this pattern. In these examples, clients can occupy the perpetrator, victim, and rescuer positions when they harm themselves and then take care of their injury.
- Re-enactments are a brilliant attempt to achieve mastery over a painful past experience or to stay safe in relationships. Be curious about the function of roles (e.g., "How did this pattern help you survive a difficult childhood?").
- After acknowledging the protective function of the behavior, it might also be useful to explore the costs (e.g., "Are there ways this is interfering now?").

References

Karpman, Stephen. 1968. "Fairy Tales and Script Drama Analysis." *Transactional Analysis Bulletin* 7(26): 39–43.

———. 2014. *A Game Free Life: The New Transactional Analysis of Intimacy, Openness, and Happiness.* San Francisco: Drama Triangle Publications.

———. 2019. *Collected Papers in Transactional Analysis.* San Francisco: Drama Triangle Publications.

KARPMAN'S TRIANGLE

This model helps us understand common unhealthy relational patterns and conflicts that arise in everyday life. By exploring the unmet needs in each of the roles depicted in the triangle, we can begin to identify ways to change these patterns and step out of the triangle.

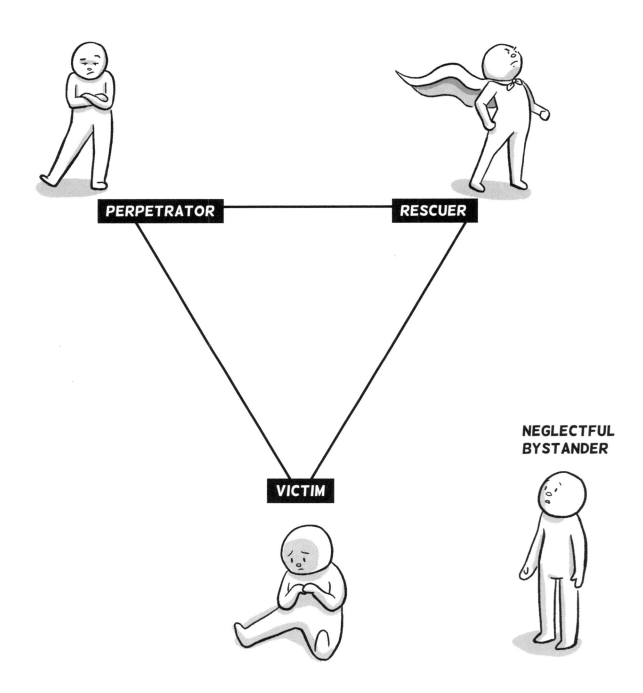

Adapted from Karpman, Stephen. 2014. *A Game Free Life: The New Transactional Analysis of Intimacy, Openness, and Happiness.* San Francisco: Drama Triangle Publications.

KARPMAN'S TRIANGLE: STEPPING OUT

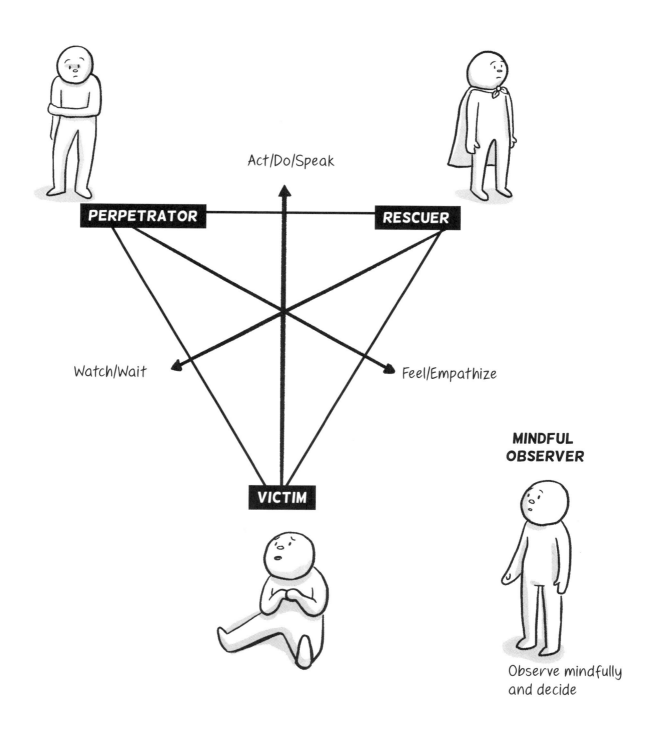

Act/Do/Speak

PERPETRATOR — RESCUER

Watch/Wait

Feel/Empathize

VICTIM

MINDFUL OBSERVER

Observe mindfully and decide

Adapted from Karpman, Stephen. 2014. *A Game Free Life: The New Transactional Analysis of Intimacy, Openness, and Happiness.* San Francisco: Drama Triangle Publications.

Chapter 11

Roles and Re-enactments Hexagon

Sue MacRae

Background

The hexagon model is based on original work by Jon Allen, a therapist and scholar in the area of trauma and relationships. This particular model is focused on the concept of re-enactments, or the tendency for "individuals who have undergone trauma in earlier relationships to recreate it unwittingly in later relationships" (Allen 2005, 180).

Allen used this model to juxtapose relational patterns that evolve as coping strategies in the context of abuse with relational patterns that happen in the context of day-to-day interactions. He helped clients explore how "ordinary interactions can evoke traumatic levels of responsiveness, because they may constitute reminders of the trauma" (Allen 2001, 76).

How to Use This Model

Step 1: Understanding the Outer Hexagon
The outer hexagon represents everyday life experiences and behaviors that we cannot avoid. All people experience a range of positive and negative life events and behaviors. As humans, we can feel helped or hurt by others and we can be helping or hurtful toward others (Allen 2005).

Describe the active and passive pairs of everyday experiences and behavior on the outer hexagon and provide examples:

- Helped and helping: For example, you can be helped by others by allowing them to offer you empathy, support, or practical help, and you can be helpful to yourself by eating well, hydrating, and getting enough sleep.
- Ignored and ignoring: For example, you can be ignored by others when they are preoccupied, distant, or detached, or you may be ignoring someone else if you are too busy to answer the phone or have to focus on other priorities.
- Hurt and hurting: For example, you can feel hurt or disappointed when someone is not attuned to your feelings. You can hurt others by missing an event you promised to attend.

Step 2: Understanding the Inner Hexagon
The inner hexagon represents a template or "blueprint" of traumatic experiences from the past.

- Validate how trauma survivors, in response to abuse and neglect, have experienced intense feelings and reactions and have often had to respond by using extreme behaviors to cope.
- Describe the active and passive pairs of experience and behavior on the inner hexagon and provide examples.

Step 3: Re-enactments

Re-enactments are unprocessed experiences from the past that intrude into the present, resulting in a repetition of unhealthy relationship patterns. A trauma survivor may notice a re-enactment when ordinary interactions evoke a disproportionate response or behavior.

Review the most common re-enactment examples, where everyday experiences on the outer hexagon are experienced as traumatic or dangerous. For example:

- Helped becomes rescued: An experience of wanting help becomes an exaggerated hope for rescue. For example, someone may hope or expect to be rescued from childhood feelings of worthlessness, hopelessness, or actual life circumstances by a partner, a parent, or a therapist. Or a person may feel overly indebted to someone who has helped them.
- Helping becomes rescuing: The natural impulse to help someone shifts into an effort to rescue them. This includes offering to others what a person needs for themselves or giving so much to others that the person feels depleted and cannot attend to their own self-care.
- Ignored becomes neglected: An experience of being ignored activates a blueprint of being neglected. For example, accusing a partner or friend of neglect when they don't respond to a text message during a busy workday.
- Ignoring becomes neglecting: Making a choice to disengage temporarily feels neglectful. For example, not responding to friend's phone call or text right away, or asking your child to wait because you are busy, feels neglectful—as though you are causing harm to this person.
- Hurt becomes abused: Mistaking hurtful behavior from others as abuse. For example, a friend says they "don't care for" your haircut and you respond by telling them they are being abusive.
- Hurting becomes abusing: An experience of mistaking your own behavior as abusive when, in fact, you have hurt another person. For example, avoiding telling someone that you are not interested in dating them because you imagine they will experience you as abusive.

There is another type of re-enactment where the traumatic experience or behavior is minimized into an everyday occurrence. For example:

- Abuse minimized to hurt: A trauma survivor is so accustomed to abuse that they mistake it as reasonable behavior or less dangerous than it really is. Some people might find it difficult to imagine a different narrative for themselves and stay in violent relationships as a familiar pattern.
- Abusing minimized as hurting: A person spanks their child regularly and states, "Discipline is good for kids. That's how I was raised, and I turned out okay."
- Rescuing minimized to helping: A person sacrifices their own life and well-being to help their parents despite ongoing abuse and states, "It is my duty to help them and I am fine."
- Neglecting minimized to ignoring: A person neglects seeking medical care and states that their foot has been "a bit sore" after a fall. The foot is swollen, bruised, and turns out to be broken.

Step 4: Working with Re-enactments

- Explain that in this model, re-enactments are more likely to occur when the space between the inner and outer hexagon is narrow. When the space between the outer and inner hexagon is wide, similar to a wide window of tolerance (see chapter 4), there is an ability to separate day-to-day reactions from trauma responses. This allows more choice and contributes to a greater sense of personal empowerment.
- Brainstorm an example, with the client or group, of a re-enactment along the continuum from day-to-day experience to re-experiencing trauma.
- Ask client(s) to describe their feelings, sensations, thoughts, and impulses as they move from present (outer hexagon) to past (inner hexagon)—for example, from helping to rescuing.
- As home practice, encourage client(s) to explore the other re-enactments that are meaningful for them as well.
- Ask client(s) to write or draw strategies that help them stay present and widen the space between the inner and outer hexagon.

Educational Gems

- It is important to remain non-judgmental when discussing experiences on the inner hexagon and re-enactments.
- Remind clients that children use the best options they have available to survive trauma. Having compassion for particular experiences, behaviors, and reactions helps widen the distance between the inner and outer hexagon, increasing options for healing.
- It is helpful to start with the rescued/rescuing examples, move to the neglected/neglecting pairs, and then the abused/abusing pairs. Following this order seems to be least activating for clients.

References

Allen, Jon G. 2001. *Traumatic Relationships and Serious Mental Disorders*. Rexdale, ON: John Wiley and Sons.

———. 2005. *Coping with Trauma: Hope Through Understanding*. Arlington, VA: American Psychiatric Publishing.

HEXAGON MODEL: RELATIONSHIP ROLES AND RE-ENACTMENTS

The hexagon model helps us understand how childhood trauma can impact relationships in adulthood.

OUTER HEXAGON

The outer hexagon represents everyday life experiences with other people that we can't avoid. As humans, we not only help each other but also hurt each other.

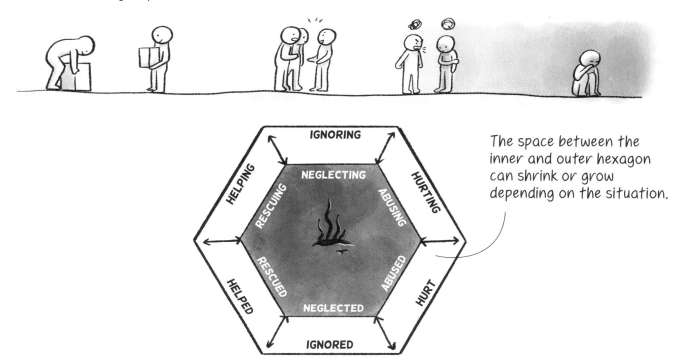

The space between the inner and outer hexagon can shrink or grow depending on the situation.

INNER HEXAGON

The inner hexagon represents a template or "blueprint" of traumatic experiences from the past.

RE-ENACTMENTS

Re-enactments are unprocessed experiences from the past that intrude into the present, resulting in a repetition of unhealthy relationship patterns. For example, a person might mistake abuse as a reasonable behavior, or a person experiencing hurt in a relationship might mistake this for abuse. In this model, re-enactments are represented by the narrowing of the space between the inner and outer hexagon.

Adapted from Allen, Jon G. 2001. *Traumatic Relationships and Serious Mental Disorders*. Rexdale, ON: John Wiley and Sons. Copyright © 2001 by John Wiley & Sons Ltd.

WORKING WITH RE-ENACTMENTS

Below is an example of a common re-enactment along the helping and rescuing continuum. What are your feelings, sensations, thoughts, and impulses as you move between these positions on the hexagon?

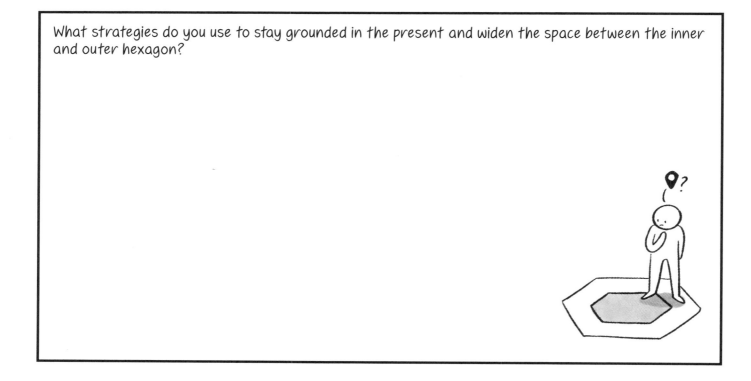

HELPING

RESCUING

What strategies do you use to stay grounded in the present and widen the space between the inner and outer hexagon?

Chapter 12

Relationship Grid

Tessa Colthoff

Background

The relationship grid is a tool developed by Terrence Real, a family therapist and founder of the Relational Life Institute. This model is used to understand relationship dynamics along the continuums of self-esteem and boundaries. It can be particularly useful to help people reflect on how their childhood experiences (including trauma) have impacted these concepts. The intention of this model is to help people identify their adaptive and maladaptive relationship patterns, or "relational edges," and explore strategies for shifting patterns that are no longer useful by promoting movement in the direction of the "circle of health."

How to Use This Model

This model can be used with couples, with individuals, or in a group therapy setting. It is useful when clients are interested in understanding their recurring relational dynamics. It is important to note that the quadrants depicted in the comic represent behavioral states rather than personal traits.

Start by providing psychoeducation about the concepts of self-esteem and boundaries and how these are shaped by experiences from the past.

Step 1: What Is Self-Esteem?

Start by describing the concept of self-esteem.

· Healthy self-esteem means holding yourself in warm regard despite your imperfections: "I am enough, and I matter." It is the belief that you have inherent worth just because you are a living, breathing human being.

Internally driven self-esteem:

· Comes from the inside, cannot be added to or subtracted from. Your worth cannot be more or less than that of any other person. It is about being, not doing, and your self-worth doesn't change over time. You are the "same as" the other, and the other is the "same as" you.
· Individuals who have experienced trauma have often had limited opportunities to foster internally driven self-esteem.
· Adding to the challenge, North American culture relies on externally driven self-esteem.

- Shifting to an internally driven self-esteem framework is possible but requires mindful presence, as it is a bold shift from mainstream culture.

Externally driven self-esteem:
- Comes from the outside, can be added to or subtracted from. Your worth is dependent on your performance (e.g., work, school, sports), what you have/own (e.g., car, home, clothes, electronics), or what others think of you.
- Externally driven self-esteem is very fragile: you are only as worthy as your last performance, your latest purchase, or other people's approval.
- Western culture tends to value external markers of "success," which contributes to all-or-nothing thinking or a winner-loser mentality.

Use the comic to show self-esteem as an energy that exists on a continuum from inferiority to superiority.
- Too much self-esteem leads to an inflated sense of self (e.g., one-up or superiority).
- Too little self-esteem leads to a deflated sense of self (e.g., one-down or inferiority).

Another way to explain the inferiority-superiority continuum is by describing the energy of contempt, which is a strong feeling of disdain or dislike toward something or someone. This energy can go in two directions:
- Contempt toward others is the same as superiority or grandiosity.
- Contempt toward self is the same as inferiority, toxic shame, and/or guilt.

Step 2: What Are Boundaries?

Start by describing the concept of boundaries.
- Differentiate between physical and psychological boundaries.
- Having a physical boundary means that you respect the physical and bodily space of others and you insist that they respect yours.
- Having a psychological boundary means that there is a separation between you and the rest of the world.
- Psychological boundaries have two functions: protection and containment. The protective boundary shields you from the world, while the containing boundary shields the world from you.
- The containing boundary is your capacity for restraint.
- A person's boundary style is not always set and can jump from one extreme to the other or hold multiple experiences at once (see chapter 9). For example, an individual might pursue someone endlessly and withdraw the moment they are noticed.

Table 12.1 | Examples of superiority, inferiority, and healthy self-esteem

Superiority	Inferiority	Healthy self-esteem
I am above the rules.	I am below the rules.	I respect the rules and I am worthy of being treated by the rules.
You are worthless.	I am worthless.	I am worthy; you are worthy.
My truth is the truth.	My truth is not worthy of being heard or listened to.	I have my truth and you have yours. Both are valid whether I agree with yours or not.

Use the comic to show that boundaries exist on a continuum from "walled off" to "boundaryless."

Walled-off boundaries:
- When you live behind a fortress of walls, you are very well protected but not connected.
- People use walls to protect themselves. These walls might be expressed as: walls of anger, words, silence, intoxication, preoccupation, charm, humor, helplessness, fatigue, or screen time.
- Someone with a walled-off boundary may be experienced by others as disconnected, uncaring, procrastinating, aloof, disinterested, or cold.
- They may not be interested in contact, or don't know how to make contact, while relying on self-soothing techniques, distractions, or addictions.
- Note: a walled-off boundary style is appropriate when you are being abused and cannot get away.

Boundaryless:
- When you adopt a porous or non-existent protective boundary, you are overly connected to internal and external experiences without protection.
- Someone with a boundaryless style may be experienced by others as thin-skinned, reactive, or overly sensitive.
- They may try to control or change the external world in an attempt to feel protected, and they might over-share their feelings and ideas.
- Someone with a boundaryless style might be experienced by others as intrusive or engulfing.
- They might have difficulty stopping inappropriate impulses, such as aggressive behavior, wanting to be right, or controlling others.
- Ask your client(s) which boundary style they can identify with, or if they identify with one boundary style more than the other. What does it look and feel like when you are walled off or boundaryless? What are your emotions, sensations, thoughts, and behaviors?

Step 3: The Circle of Health

Signs that individuals are in their circle of health include, but are not limited to:
- Compassion.
- Respect.
- Warmth.
- Acknowledgment.
- Relaxation.
- Humility.
- The ability to give and receive.

Skills in the circle of health include:
- Listening to understand vs. listening to respond.
- Empowering yourself and others.
- Making requests vs. complaining.
- Taking responsibility for your own behaviors and feelings.

Practicing healthy self-esteem:
- Healthy self-esteem lies within the circle of health, between superiority and inferiority.
- It is normal and healthy to feel good about yourself when you do well. This feeling serves as an internal motivator—like a gas pedal—and increases the likelihood that you will repeat the behavior in future. On the flip side, appropriate and healthy shame serves as the internal brake system when you engage in unfavorable behavior, and it will decrease the likelihood that you will repeat the behavior in future.
- Ask client(s) to notice when they find themselves outside of the circle of health. What emotions, physical sensations, thoughts, and behaviors do they notice?

- Ask client(s): What are the signs that they are inside the circle of health and practicing healthy self-esteem?

Practicing healthy boundaries:
- Healthy boundaries lie within the circle of health, between walled-off and boundaryless.
- The goal is to be able to appropriately lean into or lean out of connection with others without finding yourself in the extremes.
- When you have functional or flexible boundaries, you are protected and connected at the same time. Intimacy and connection can thrive when you have healthy boundaries.
- Ask your client(s) to notice when they find themselves outside of the circle of health. What emotions, physical sensations, thoughts, and behaviors do they notice?
- Ask client(s): What are the signs that they are inside the circle of health and practicing healthy boundaries?

Educational Gems
- A person's boundary style is informed by their upbringing. Children are shown how to use and adapt their boundaries in different situations by modeling and responding to their caregivers. These adaptive strategies become hardwired and feel like "the way we are."
- A person's self-esteem is also influenced by their upbringing. When caregivers are limited in their ability to mirror and reflect their child's inherent worth, they are likely to seek reassurance and validation externally.
- Offer validation that these adaptive stances were once functional and crucial to their safety and survival.

- Explore how their ways of being in relationship connect to their past (e.g., What were your caregivers' boundary styles? Which boundary style did you rely on as a child? How was self-esteem fostered growing up? In what quadrant did your caregivers' behaviors fit?).
- Ask client(s) if they can identify their relational edges and patterns. Do they tend to identify with one quadrant, or do they move between quadrants?
- Brainstorm ways to recognize when their adaptive stances are activated.
- Ask client(s) if different relational stances get activated with different people. Is there a "type" of person that triggers a certain reaction? Who does this person represent from your past?
- Ask client(s) to reflect on a recent interaction where they felt activated. Where did they go on the grid?
- Remind clients that the initial aim is to become aware of behavioral patterns that lead to unhealthy relational dynamics. Then, like a muscle, healthy self-esteem and boundaries need to be exercised to get strong. This is a learning process which will take time.
- Brainstorm outcome strategies to move back into the circle of health by practicing healthy self-esteem and boundaries.

References
Real, Terrence. 2008. *The New Rules of Marriage: What You Need to Know to Make Love Work*. New York: Ballantine Books.

Table 12.2 | Tips: Practicing healthy self-esteem and boundaries

Superiority / One-Up and Walled Off "You're not worthy of my love"	Superiority / One-Up and Boundaryless "Love me or else"
Avoid • Using contempt by putting others down or shaming them • Holding on to grudges • Entitlement/being mean • Meeting harshness with harshness • Giving others the cold shoulder/silent treatment • Withholding as punishment Try • Breathing yourself down to "same as" others' position • Reminding yourself that you are not worth more than others • Softening your relational edges and coming back into connection • Working through resentment • Leading with what you can give	Avoid • Using contempt toward others through violence, abuse, or disrespectful behavior • Controlling others directly (e.g., commanding) or indirectly (e.g., manipulation) • Using unbridled self-expression (e.g., venting, bringing up every past offense into an argument) Try • Breathing yourself down to "same as" others' position • Reminding yourself that you are not worth more than others • Practicing restraint (e.g., adjusting volume and tone of voice, and speaking from the "I") • Making room for differences instead of wanting to be right
Inferiority / One-Down and Walled Off **"I'm not worthy of your love"**	**Inferiority / One-Down and Boundaryless** **"I'll do anything for love"**
Avoid • Accepting contempt by putting up with disrespectful behavior • Accepting your "fate" and staying silent • Shutting down and withdrawing • Behaviors that promote avoidance (e.g., internet, gaming, substances) Try • Breathing yourself up to "same as" others' position • Reminding yourself that you are not worth less than others • Taking space in healthy ways • Re-engaging with others • Activating yourself into connection • Taking risks • Reaching out and accepting help	Avoid • Accepting contempt out of fear of loss or feeling unworthy • Unbridled self-expression (e.g., excessive sharing) • Taking things personally • Acting from desperation and urgency • Controlling others • Retaliating or offending from the victim position • Hurting others because they hurt you Try • Breathing yourself up to "same as" others' position • Reminding yourself that you are not worth less than others • Slowing things down • Using soothing strategies to lower urgency • Practicing restraint (e.g., limit excessive sharing) • Asserting boundaries and saying no • Speaking up when treated with disrespect • Reaching out to people who can help • Considering ways to strengthen your protective boundary

RELATIONSHIP GRID

This model helps us understand how self-esteem and boundaries affect our relationship with ourselves and others.

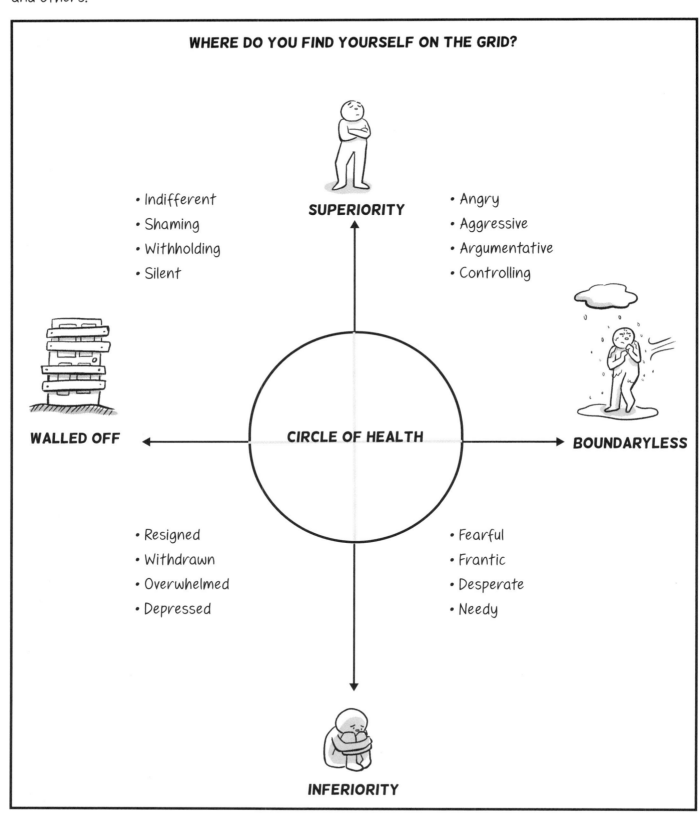

WHERE DO YOU FIND YOURSELF ON THE GRID?

SUPERIORITY

- Indifferent
- Shaming
- Withholding
- Silent

- Angry
- Aggressive
- Argumentative
- Controlling

WALLED OFF

CIRCLE OF HEALTH

BOUNDARYLESS

- Resigned
- Withdrawn
- Overwhelmed
- Depressed

- Fearful
- Frantic
- Desperate
- Needy

INFERIORITY

© 2020 Trauma Education Comics, P. Nguyen, L. Hughes and A. Hershler
Contributing author T. Colthoff
Adapted from Real, Terrence. 2008. *The New Rules of Marriage: What You Need to Know to Make Love Work*. New York: Ballantine Books.

LIVING RELATIONALLY

Pause for a moment to locate yourself on the grid.
You can use this information to guide you closer to the circle of health.

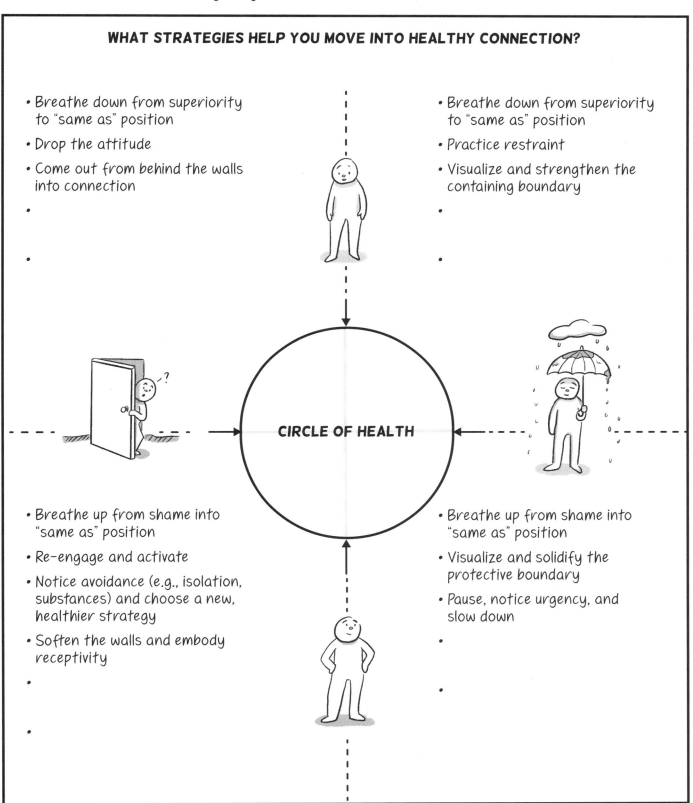

WHAT STRATEGIES HELP YOU MOVE INTO HEALTHY CONNECTION?

- Breathe down from superiority to "same as" position
- Drop the attitude
- Come out from behind the walls into connection
-
-

- Breathe down from superiority to "same as" position
- Practice restraint
- Visualize and strengthen the containing boundary
-
-

CIRCLE OF HEALTH

- Breathe up from shame into "same as" position
- Re-engage and activate
- Notice avoidance (e.g., isolation, substances) and choose a new, healthier strategy
- Soften the walls and embody receptivity
-
-

- Breathe up from shame into "same as" position
- Visualize and solidify the protective boundary
- Pause, notice urgency, and slow down
-
-

MOVING AHEAD

Thank you for traveling on this path of self-reflection and growth.

You are on your way and the journey continues.

FEAR
ANGER
GROWTH
HESITATION
SELF-REFLECTION

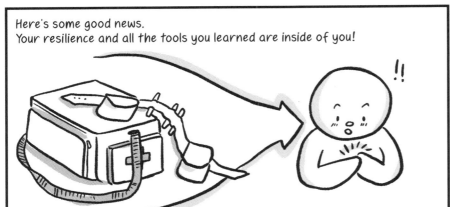

Here's some good news.
Your resilience and all the tools you learned are inside of you!

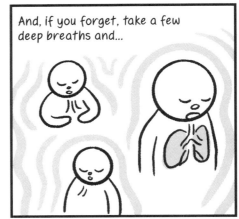

And, if you forget, take a few deep breaths and...

... come back to these comics and remind yourself that these skills require lifelong practice.

Sometimes life may present obstacles...

... and other times you may catch your stride!

WOO!

About the Contributors

Tessa Colthoff (Drs. C. Psych. Assoc.) is a psychological associate registered with the College of Psychologists of Ontario. Her clinical area of interest is working with adult survivors of childhood trauma, war, and organized and systemic violence. She is a certified couples therapist with the Relational Life Institute. Tessa provides individual, group, and couples therapy in the Trauma Therapy Program at Women's College Hospital (Toronto, Canada) and sees individuals and couples in her private practice. In addition to her clinical work, she is engaged in several research initiatives.

Marlene Duarte Giles (MSW, RSW) is a social worker/psychotherapist with the Trauma Therapy Program and Women Recovering from Abuse Program (WRAP) at Women's College Hospital (Toronto, Canada). Marlene works as a group and individual therapist, with expertise in therapy for individuals who have experienced childhood trauma. In addition to her clinical work, she teaches as an adjunct lecturer within the Factor-Inwentash Faculty of Social Work as well as the Department of Psychiatry at the University of Toronto. She has published in the *Journal of Trauma and Dissociation* related to her work in WRAP. Marlene is most uplifted when she is creating—favoring drawing and curating interior spaces. She also relishes spending time with her family, surrounded by nature, in all seasons.

Abby Hershler (MD, MA, FRCPC) is a staff psychiatrist at Women's College Hospital (Toronto, Canada), dividing her time between the Trauma Therapy and General Psychiatry teams, as well as the Women Recovering from Abuse Program (WRAP). She provides consultation support and collaborative care to Crossroads Refugee Clinic at Women's College Hospital and Native Men's Residence shelter through Inner City Health Associates. In her role as assistant professor in the Department of Psychiatry at the University of Toronto, she greatly enjoys supervising residents and medical students in psychiatric care and psychotherapy. She has a particular interest in relational and trauma-focused individual and group psychotherapy, as well as the role of art in healing.

Lesley Hughes (MSW, RSW) is a registered social worker. Her clinical specialty is working with adults who have experienced childhood trauma in the Trauma Therapy Program and the Women Recovering from Abuse Program (WRAP) at Women's College Hospital (Toronto, Canada). Lesley is an adjunct lecturer at the Factor-Inwentash Faculty of Social Work at the University of Toronto, where she provides clinical supervision and education to graduate students. Lesley is keenly interested in the relationship between trauma and the body. As a certified yoga instructor with training in sensorimotor psychotherapy, she has combined these interests to pilot trauma-informed mindful movement groups. Lesley is equally committed to engaging in research initiatives, having recently published in the *Journal of Trauma and Dissociation*.

Janet Lee-Evoy (MD, FRCPC) is a staff psychiatrist at Women's College Hospital (Toronto, Canada) and a lecturer in the Department of Psychiatry at the University of Toronto. She works on the Trauma Therapy and General Psychiatry teams and provides collaborative care and consultation to the Crossroads Refugee Clinic at Women's College Hospital, the Centre for Headache at Women's College Hospital, and YWCA supportive housing in Toronto.

Sue MacRae (RN, MEd, RP) is a registered nurse and psychotherapist. Sue currently works full-time in Toronto at Women's College Hospital in the Women Recovering from Abuse Program (WRAP) and the Trauma Therapy Program. She has expertise in both group and individual therapy modalities. Sue has published and lectured extensively on topics related to clinical bioethics, relationship-centered care, and psychotherapy in the context of childhood trauma. Sue also has a psychotherapy private practice and is an adjunct professor in the Dalla Lana School of Public Health at the University of Toronto.

Nancy McCallum (MD, MSc, FRCPC) is a staff psychiatrist at Women's College Hospital (Toronto, Canada), and the program lead for the Trauma Therapy Program (TTP). She provides individual and group psychotherapy in the TTP and Women Recovering from Abuse Program (WRAP), and she is trained in a variety of treatment modalities, including sensorimotor psychotherapy, internal family systems, and neurofeedback. As an assistant professor of psychiatry at the University of Toronto, she supervises resident students in trauma-focused psychiatric care and psychotherapy and participates in research in trauma treatment. She loves the connection and collaboration of teams, including being on the amazing TTP team as well as a swimmer/volunteer/parent with the Toronto Artistic Swimming Club, and part of a fabulous family as daughter, sister, wife, and mom of the two best kids ever.

Holly Miles (RP) is a psychotherapist at Women's College Hospital (Toronto, Canada). Holly works in the Trauma Therapy Program and the Reproductive Life Stages Program, with a focus on supporting patients with trauma histories during the peripartum period. She incorporates narrative therapy, mindfulness, and expressive arts therapy in her approach within a feminist anti-oppressive framework.

Mahum Musheer (MEd, RP) is a registered psychotherapist. Her clinical specialty is working with adults who have experienced interpersonal childhood trauma as well as with adults who struggle with substance use. Mahum is currently working in the Trauma Therapy Program and the Women Recovering from Abuse Program (WRAP) at Women's College Hospital (Toronto, Canada). In addition to her clinical work, Mahum also provides supervision and education to graduate students from the University of Toronto.

She has specialized training in sensorimotor psychotherapy and has a particular interest in relational psychotherapy.

Patricia Nguyen (BScKin, MScBMC) is a medical illustrator who studied in the Biomedical Communications program at the University of Toronto. She works as a medical illustrator, creating educational medical videos at a medical and health sciences education technology company. She is interested in the use of graphic medicine as a means to explain abstract and emotional concepts in the context of mental health and patient education.

Meaghan Peckham (MSW, RSW) is a social worker/psychotherapist in the Trauma Therapy Program at Women's College Hospital (Toronto, Canada). She is an adjunct lecturer in the Factor-Inwentash Faculty of Social Work at the University of Toronto and provides clinical supervision to graduate students. In addition to her part-time work at Women's College Hospital, she also works in her private practice to provide psychotherapy to individuals and couples. She specializes in trauma recovery and interpersonal relational challenges, with a particular focus on clients in the LGBTQI2S+ community.

Susshma Persaud (MSW, RSW) is a social worker/psychotherapist who practices in the Trauma Therapy Program at Women's College Hospital (Toronto, Ontario). She is an adjunct lecturer at the University of Toronto in the Faculty of Social Work. Susshma's area of expertise is trauma-focused individual and group therapy, and she has specialized training in sensorimotor psychotherapy and internal family systems. She facilitates trauma training workshops online and in the community. Susshma completed her

Master of Social Work degree from the University of Toronto and has worked in the Trauma Therapy Program at Women's College Hospital since 2007.

Eva-Marie Stern (MA, RP) is an art therapist, psychotherapist, and educator. As adjunct faculty in the Department of Psychiatry at the University of Toronto, she consults, writes, and offers seminars that catalyze art as a medium for learning about relationships, trauma, health, and humanness. She co-founded the Women Recovering from Abuse Program and the Trauma Therapy Program at Women's College Hospital (Toronto, Canada) and currently works from her therapy studio, https://www.artandmind.net.

Shelley Wall (AOCAD, MScBMC, PhD) is an associate professor in the Biomedical Communications graduate program at the University of Toronto. Her primary area of research and creation is graphic medicine—that is, comics as a medium for narratives of health and illness. In addition to creating her own comics and collaborating with others to tell their stories visually, she teaches a graduate course on graphic medicine within the Institute of Medical Science, University of Toronto, and offers seminars in graphic medicine and illustration as a means of reflection for medical students, interprofessional education classes, and medical practitioners.